THE MEMORANDA OF UNDERSTANDING BETWEEN THE U.S. AND CHINA REGARDING PRISON LABOR

HEARING

BEFORE THE

U.S.-CHINA ECONOMIC AND SECURITY REVIEW COMMISSION

ONE HUNDRED TENTH CONGRESS

SECOND SESSION

———————

JUNE 19, 2008

———————

Printed for use of the

United States-China Economic and Security Review Commission
Available via the World Wide Web: www.uscc.gov

UNITED STATES-CHINA ECONOMIC AND SECURITY REVIEW COMMISSION

WASHINGTON : JULY 2008

U.S.-CHINA ECONOMIC AND SECURITY REVIEW COMMISSION

LARRY M. WORTZEL, *Chairman*
CAROLYN BARTHOLOMEW, *Vice Chairman*

Commissioners:

PETER T.R. BROOKES   Hon. WILLIAM A. REINSCH
DANIEL BLUMENTHAL   Hon. DENNIS C. SHEA
MARK ESPER   DANIEL M. SLANE
JEFFREY FIEDLER   PETER VIDENIEKS
Hon. PATRICK A. MULLOY   MICHAEL R. WESSEL

T. SCOTT BUNTON, *Executive Director*
KATHLEEN J. MICHELS, *Associate Director*

The Commission was created on October 30, 2000 by the Floyd D. Spence National Defense Authorization Act for 2001 § 1238, Public Law No. 106-398, 114 STAT. 1654A-334 (2000) (codified at 22 U.S.C.§ 7002 (2001), as amended by the Treasury and General Government Appropriations Act for 2002 § 645 (regarding employment status of staff) & § 648 (regarding changing annual report due date from March to June), Public Law No. 107-67, 115 STAT. 514 (Nov. 12, 2001); as amended by Division P of the "Consolidated Appropriations Resolution, 2003," Pub L. No. 108-7 (Feb. 20, 2003) (regarding Commission name change, terms of Commissioners, and responsibilities of Commission); as amended by Public Law No. 109-108 (H.R. 2862) (Nov. 22, 2005) (regarding responsibilities of Commission and applicability of FACA); as amended by Division J of the "Consolidated Appropriations Act, 2008, "Public Law No. 110-161 (December 26, 2007) (regarding responsibilities of the Commission, and changing the Annual Report due date from June to December).

The Commission's full charter is available at www.uscc.gov.

CONTENTS

_____

THURSDAY, JUNE 19, 2008

THE MEMORANDA OF UNDERSTANDING BETWEEN THE U.S. AND CHINA REGARDING PRISON LABOR PRODUCTS

PANEL I: THE STATE OF PRISON LABOR IN CHINA'S PRISON SYSTEM

PANEL II: THE STATE OF CHINESE COMPLIANCE WITH THE PRISON LABOR MOU/ADMINISTRATION PERSPECTIVES

July 31, 2008

The Honorable ROBERT C. BYRD
President Pro Tempore of the Senate, Washington, D.C. 20510
The Honorable NANCY PELOSI
Speaker of the House of Representatives, Washington, D.C. 20515

DEAR SENATOR BYRD AND SPEAKER PELOSI:

We are pleased to transmit the record of our June 19, 2008 public hearing on *"The Memorandum of Agreement Between the United States and China Regarding Prison Labor Products."* The Floyd D. Spence National Defense Authorization Act (amended by Pub. L. No. 109-108, section 635(a)) provides the basis for this hearing, stating that the Commission shall examine "…the degree of non-compliance by the People's Republic of China with agreements between the United States and the People's Republic of China on prison labor imports… and United States enforcement policies with respect to such agreements." The agreements in question are a 1992 Memorandum of Agreement (MOU) that prison-made products will not be exported from China to the United States, and a subsequent 1994 Statement of Cooperation (SOC) that more explicitly defines the investigation and resolution procedures for alleged cases of prison-made goods.

The hearing was organized into two panels. The first panel focused on China's prison labor system, commonly termed the *laogai* ("reform through labor"), and on the export of Chinese prison-made products to the United States. The panel featured testimony by Mr. Harry Wu, the Executive Director of the Laogai Research Foundation and himself a former political prisoner in the *laogai* system. It also featured testimony by Mr. Gary Marck, a businessman who professes first-hand knowledge of Chinese prison-made imports entering the United States, and Mr. Daniel Ellis of the law firm of Lydy & Moan in Toledo, Ohio, who is Mr. Marck's legal counsel.

Mr. Wu offered a harsh assessment of the efficacy of the 1992 MOU and the subsequent 1994 SOC, stating that "…these bilateral agreements have done little to uphold United States law or to promote the respect of human rights as a key element of U.S. foreign policy. Rather, they have only served to provide the PRC with diplomatic cover that it can use to defend itself in the face of criticism regarding the export of prison labor products." He went on to describe a long history of Chinese government obstruction of the implementation of the provisions of the MOU and SOC, including denials and lengthy delays in acting on U.S. government requests to inspect alleged prison factory facilities in accordance with the stipulations of these agreements. He also discussed a June 2008 report by the Laogai Research Foundation, titled *Laogai Forced Labor Camps Listed in Dun & Bradstreet Databases*. Mr. Wu stated that the report identifies 314 different prison facilities that are linked to commercial enterprises, thereby indicating a significant economic role for many of the prisons of the *laogai* network.

Following this, Mr. Marck and Mr. Ellis offered a case study setting out their views of how Chinese prison-made products enter the United States in violation of U.S. law, and of the ways in which this can affect American businesses. Mr. Marck, who operates a wholesaling company that markets drinkware products, is involved in ongoing litigation with a competitor whom Mr. Marck has claimed was underselling him by importing ceramic coffee mugs produced at a Chinese prison factory. Mr. Marck conducted a private investigation that he said identified the Luzhong Prison in Shandong Province as the point of origin for the mugs in question, and he further identified a company named Shandong Zibo Maolong Ceramic Factory as a "front" company for the prison's products. Mr. Marck claimed that this unfair competition had both negatively impacted his business and forced him to spend significant time and money pursuing his investigation and litigation.

Responding to questions from the Commissioners, Mr. Marck asserted that he had received very little assistance from agencies of the U.S. government, opining that U.S. Immigration and Customs Enforcement (ICE) of the Department of Homeland Security had insufficient resources and authority inside China to assist effectively with such cases. Mr. Marck and Mr. Ellis recommended that the burden of proof be shifted to U.S. importers, requiring them to certify that their imported products were not produced by prison labor. He further recommended that companies be granted a "private right of action" to pursue alleged customs violations by their competitors. Finally, he recommended that falsifications of product origin labeling be pursued and prosecuted as violations of the Lanham Act of 1947, which prohibits trademark infringement, trademark dilution, and false advertising. The Commission will conduct further research on these and other matters related to prison labor imports – particularly the recommendation of Mr. Ellis that Congress grant a "private right of action" – in order to more fully understand the complexities of these issues prior to providing policy recommendations in its annual report later this year.

The second panel examined the state of Chinese government compliance with the provisions of the 1992 MOU and 1994 SOC, and whether any changes to those instruments might be needed. This panel featured the testimony of Mr. James Ink, Deputy Assistant Director of the Office of International Affairs, ICE. (ICE is the federal agency that has been given primary responsibility for working with Chinese officials to investigate and resolve alleged cases of prison labor goods exported to the United States, although Customs and Border Protection (CBP) would be the responsible agency for actually issuing detention orders against any manufacturers identified as being involved in such activity.) The Commission also was very interested in having a representative of the U.S. State Department speak to the diplomatic aspects of this issue. Regrettably, however, despite repeated invitations extended through both informal and formal channels, the State Department declined to send a representative to participate in the hearing.

Although he did not directly characterize it as such, both Mr. Ink's prepared statement and his answers to Commissioners' questions revealed that Chinese government cooperation with the United States to fulfill the requirements of the MOU and SOC pertaining to prison labor products has been very poor. The 1994 SOC stipulates that "…if the United States government, in order to resolve specific outstanding cases, requests a visit to a suspected facility, the Chinese government will, in conformity with Chinese laws and regulations and in accordance with the MOU, arrange for responsible United States diplomatic mission officials to visit the suspected facility within 60 days of the receipt of a written request." However, Mr. Ink indicated that there are currently 13 outstanding requests by ICE officials for on-site inspections of alleged prison labor facilities, dating back to 1994. He also indicated that contacts between representatives of China's Ministry of Justice and ICE representatives in China have been sporadic in recent years. He stated that contacts halted in 2003 in the wake of the outbreak of Severe Acute Respiratory Syndrome (SARS), resumed from 2004 to 2006, stopped again for two years, and only resumed in June 2008. In response to Commissioners' questions, Mr. Ink also acknowledged that ICE maintains no central database of alleged prison labor product cases, but stated that local ICE offices maintain greater awareness of such issues within their geographical areas of concern. When asked directly whether he regards the prison labor MOU and SOC as effective, Mr. Ink responded that they could be if the 60-day timeframe for site inspections were actually observed, and he recommended continued diplomatic engagement as the best means to pursue progress on this issue. When asked whether or not he believes that private business interests should be granted a private right of action – as recommended by Mr. Ellis – Mr. Ink demurred, but suggested that private sector businesspeople could provide information to ICE that ICE could use to take action through government channels.

The prepared statements of the hearing witnesses can be found on the Commission's website at www.uscc.gov, and the complete hearing transcript also will be made available on the website. Members of the Commission are available to provide more detailed briefings. We hope the information from this hearing will be helpful as the Congress continues its assessment of U.S.-China relations. In its 2008 Annual Report that will be submitted to Congress in November 2008, the Commission will examine in greater depth these and the other issues enumerated in its statutory mandate.

Sincerely yours,

Larry M. Wortzel
Chairman

Carolyn Bartholomew
Vice Chairman

cc: Members of Congress and Congressional Staff

THE MEMORANDA OF UNDERSTANDING BETWEEN THE U.S. AND CHINA REGARDING PRISON LABOR PRODUCTS

———————

THURSDAY, JUNE 19, 2008

U.S. CHINA ECONOMIC AND SECURITY REVIEW COMMISSION

Washington, D.C.

The Commission met in Room 418, Russell Senate Office Building at 8:55 a.m., Chairman Larry M. Wortzel and Commissioner Peter Videnieks (Hearing Cochairs), presiding.

OPENING STATEMENT OF COMMISSIONER PETER VIDENIEKS HEARING COCHAIR

COMMISSIONER VIDENIEKS: We'd like to start the hearing now. The hearing is going to be on the Memoranda of Agreement Between the United States and China Regarding Prison Labor Products.

I'd like to welcome everybody here and to extend a special note of thanks to Chairman Akaka and members of his staff of the Senate Veterans Affairs Committee for providing us with the use of their hearing room for today's proceedings.

The continuing importation into the United States of products produced by prison labor remains a topic of serious concern to many in both Congress and the broader public. Although formal agreements have been made between the U.S. and Chinese governments to stop the export of prison labor goods to the U.S., the practice nonetheless continues.

Officials who deal with prison labor issues in the U.S. Embassy in China have recently identified a number of products produced for retail sale by prison labor, including artificial flowers, Christmas decorations, shoes and garments.

At least some of these items are making their way into the U.S. market and two of our witnesses here today will illustrate a case study of how illicit prison labor goods are making their way to American store shelves. This practice not only provides a powerful financial incentive for officials who control prison labor facilities to continue and expand such production, but also hurts legitimate U.S. businesspeople who are trying to play by the rules.

One of the main reasons that information on Chinese prison labor goods is limited is due to the fact that the Chinese government treats such information as a state secret. The Chinese government also has a very questionable record of compliance with its agreements related to prison labor products.

U.S. officials attempting to implement the provisions of these agreements have described China as a challenging operating environment and have often found their Chinese counterparts to be either unresponsive or actually obstructive.

Today, we will be examining the overall state of the Chinese government compliance with the provisions from the 1992 and 1994 agreements related to prison labor products, and seeking greater clarity on the issue as we consider the policy recommendations that we will present to Congress later in the year.

I would like to introduce the panelists, and the questions will be addressed in that order.

Mr. Harry Wu is an American activist for human rights in the People's Republic of China. He's now a citizen of the United States and Mr. Wu spent 19 years in Chinese labor camps for which he popularized the term "laogai." He established the Laogai Research Foundation, a nonprofit research and public education organization.

Second would be Mr. Gary G. Marck. Mr. Marck is President of G.G. Marck & Associates, an importer and distributor of drinkware products with offices and warehouses in Toledo, Ohio and Mira Loma, California. He has worked in this industry for over 30 years and holds a number of U.S. patents for drinkware related products.

Next is Mr. Ellis, Daniel T. Ellis. He is a partner in the law firm of Lydy & Moan, Ltd., located in Sylvania, Ohio. His practice includes commercial litigation involving contract disputes, unfair competition and international trade issues for both defendants and plaintiffs.

He's also actively involved in civil rights and constitutional issues related to an individual's right to bear arms under the Ohio and U.S. Constitutions. He regularly practices in state as well as federal courts.

I'd like to now turn to Mr. Wu to begin his testimony.

STATEMENT OF MR. HARRY WU, EXECUTIVE DIRECTOR
THE LAOGAI RESEARCH FOUNDATION, WASHINGTON, D.C.

MR. WU: Thank you. It has been 16 years since the government of the United States committed itself to ensuring compliance with its own trade law with respect to the People's Republic of China. A Memorandum of Understanding, MOU, signed in 1992, and a Statement of the Cooperation, SOC, signed in 1994, were intended to provide the United States government with the tools that it needs to guarantee that products made by prison or other forced labor would not be imported into the United States from the PRC, in accordance with Section 307 of the Tariff Act of 1930, which prohibits the importation of any products made by prison labor into the United States.

Unfortunately, in my opinion, these bilateral agreements have done little to uphold United States law or to promote respect for human rights as a key element of U.S. foreign policy.

Rather, they have only served to provide the PRC with diplomatic cover that it can use to defend itself in the face of criticism regarding the export of prison labor products.

The MOU and SOC establish agreed-upon procedures for the United States to investigate allegations that such products have been imported into the country from China. Since the beginning of the fiscal year 2005, the task of investigating and enforcing laws and regulations prohibiting the importation of forced labor products into the United States has fallen under the jurisdiction of the U.S. Immigration and Customs Enforcement, ICE.

ICE can request that China investigate prison labor allegations pertaining to exports to the United States. It can request for U.S. Embassy officials to visit prisons alleged to produce products for export in order to verify that any such goods are being exported to the United States.

As of 2005, there were three officers assigned to the ICE Attaché in Beijing who were charged with conducting such investigations.

It is the duty of the U.S. Customs and Border Protection, CBP, to issue enforcement actions regarding suspected importation of prison labor products. The CBP can enter Withhold Release Orders, more commonly referred to as detention orders, when there is information available that reasonably, but not conclusively, indicates that imported merchandise has been produced with forced or indentured labor.

Subsequently, if an investigation concludes that there is probable cause that a class of merchandise, originating from a particular manufacturer, facility or distributor, is produced with forced or indentured labor, the CBP may issue a finding and entry of said merchandise is denied.

I want to give an example: the most recent investigation that was included in the report is a site visit in April 2005 conducted at the Fuyang General Machinery Factory. U.S. Embassy officials had first requested to visit this site in 1995, ten years earlier. Surely, site visits conducted a decade after information suggesting a violation had occurred was first received, and negotiated with Chinese authorities well in advance of the actual date of the visit, cannot be expected to yield any meaningful information that could be used to make a determination with respect to the allegations.

Not surprisingly, no evidence of exports to the United States of products manufactured by prison labor was found during any of the prison site visits. So this has remained an open case.

Since its founding in 1992, the Laogai Research Foundation has attempted to monitor the state of affairs in China's Laogai facilities, including the scope of their economic activity. "Laogai" literally means "reform through labor," and although the Chinese stopped using the word internally in 1994, the evidence that my foundation has gathered suggests that forced labor is as much a part of the prison system today as it ever was.

We found that more than 1,000 Laogai camps exist in China today. And recently, the Laogai Research Foundation conducted a research project to assess the degree to which products made within the Laogai are exported by China.

So we compared our Laogai Handbook with two online Dun & Bradstreet databases--Dun & Bradstreet claims to be the world's leading source of commercial information and insight on businesses-- and we found a total of 314 separate entries for Laogai camps in the Dun & Bradstreet databases. Those 314 entries in the Dun & Bradstreet databases represent 256 different Laogai camps, or approximately 25 percent of the total number of the Laogai camps identified as of 2006.

A total of 65 entries in the Dun & Bradstreet databases contain the word "prison" in their name. And the 314 entries in the Dun & Bradstreet databases include Laogai camps in 28 of 31 province level divisions.

The 314 entries for Laogai camps found in the Dun & Bradstreet databases represent 72 different products and/or product categories.

So I ask that this Commission remind our government, the United States government, that progress in this matter should not be treated as a political issue but as a legal issue. The law is clear in this matter: products produced by prison labor are prohibited from being imported into the United States regardless of the ramification that enforcement of the prohibition may have on relations with other countries. We can even go to court to sue the American government, because they did not follow the law. It is not a political issue.

So as a first step, I recommend that the MOU between the United States and the PRC be revoked, as it has been proven to be totally ineffective in providing enforcement of United States law.

Thank you.

[The statement follows:][1]

COMMISSIONER VIDENIEKS: Thank you.
Mr. Marck.

STATEMENT OF MR. GARY G. MARCK, PRESIDENT
G.G. MARCK & ASSOCIATES, INC.
TOLEDO, OHIO

MR. MARCK: Members of the Commission and staff, I would like to thank you for this opportunity to discuss the United States' relationship with the People's Republic of China as it relates to the importation of forced labor products.

My view reflects the experiences of an American importer of ceramic products with first-hand day-to-day knowledge of the ceramic industry in China and as a part owner of two ceramic factories in China. Additionally, I frequently travel to the manufacturing facilities in China to address issues related to the production and importation of ceramic products into the United States.

Specific to this hearing, I have knowledge related to the importation of ceramic coffee mugs that were made in whole or part with prison labor.

G.G. Marck & Associates was founded in 1986 to provide products to the drinkware decorating industry, mainly sold as promotional products. Marck has offices and warehouses in Toledo, Ohio and Mira Loma, California. Marck is a leading wholesaler of ceramic glass, stainless steel and plastic products to the drinkware decorating industry in the United States with over 2,000 customers.

Marck sources products domestically as well as imports from China, India, Thailand, Taiwan, Colombia, Turkey and France.

In 2004, in an effort to avoid its loss of its source of ceramic products, Marck bought a minority interest in two Chinese ceramic factories.

During this hearing, I would like to highlight the difficulties faced by U.S. companies that comply with the laws of the United

---

[1] **Click here to read the prepared statement of Mr. Harry Wu**

States by importing products from factories that do not use forced or prison labor in the production of their products.

Many foreign exporters and some U.S. importers ignore U.S. law to gain a competitive advantage, albeit an un unlawful one. The law abiding companies must choose to exit the business because the price in which the product is sold cannot be matched by lawful means or join in the unlawful importation of products from prison factories.

Additionally, the Chinese and American agencies responsible for enforcing the laws and regulations have not taken adequate measures to ensure that all competitors have met these laws and regulations.

Ultimately, without the assistance and intervention of the responsible Chinese and U.S. governmental agencies, law abiding companies, both in the U.S. and in China, will continue to go out of business and cease to exist.

The loss of these law-abiding companies impacts the United States through its loss of tax revenue and American workers because of the loss of jobs.

Marck has knowledge from a variety of sources including eyewitness evidence that ceramic coffee mugs produced at the Luzhong Prison of Shandong Province are being exported to the United States.

Since it is against Chinese laws for prison-made goods to be exported, the goods made at Luzhong need to be exported by another company. The Shandong Zibo Maolong Ceramic Factory is the front for Luzhong. Details of our investigations have been provided to the Commission.

There are two separate prison camps for Luzhong. One is for hard core, long-term prisoners, and the other is what is referred to as Re-education through Labor Facility. It may be semantics, but the Chinese do not call this a prison. It is the Re-education through Labor Facility that houses political and other petty criminals that are rehabilitated through work.

It is this Re-Education through Labor Facility that makes the ceramic coffee mugs. Maolong is a small facility just outside the main gate of Luzhong. It has limited capacity to manufacture mugs and I do not believe it has ever made mugs. It is the front company used by Luzhong to export its mugs to the United States.

In order to get these goods to the U.S., there has to be an importer. A number of U.S. importers are importing mugs made at Luzhong and exported by Maolong. Most of these importers are aware of the Luzhong-Maolong relationship but choose to ignore the fact that prison labor was used to make their mugs because of the price advantage they receive.

This relationship unlawfully benefits the three parties involved. Maolong makes profit from the export of the Luzhong mugs. Shandong

Province benefits as they make profit from the prison. Lastly, the U.S. importer that purchases the mugs from Maolong benefits from the low cost prison-made mugs.

The losers are the Chinese and U.S. companies that compete with these prison-made goods, ultimately causing the loss of jobs. China also loses as the prisons do not pay taxes as do the voluntary labor ceramic factories.

So once Maolong drives all the other ceramic factories in China out of business, they will have no tax income. Each year the number of viable manufacturing facilities declines because they can't sell their products at the same price as the prison-made products and still remain profitable.

Finally, the United States loses tax revenue directly related to the closing of businesses that cannot compete with prison-made goods.

It is Marck's belief that by increasing agency and private party remedies available, there will be significant increase in the effective enforcement of existing laws and regulations prohibiting the entry of prison-made goods into the U.S. market.

Marck submitted suggestions and concerns to this Commission on March 18, 2008, in a written statement about, quote, "China's Expanding Global Influence: Foreign Policy Goals, Practices, and Tools." A copy has been provided.

Additionally, Marck appeared before the International Trade Commission's investigation, quote, "China: Government Policies Affecting U.S. Trade in Selected Sectors," testifying to the effects of prison labor on its business and how importation of prison-made goods amounts to an unlawful government subsidy.

Marck strongly favors the recommendations made by this Commission in its May 3, 2002 letter to the Senate Finance Committee, suggesting that enforcement would be significantly enhanced by:

One, requiring the importer of record to certify that goods were not made by prison labor;

Two, by blocking imports from facilities where inspections by U.S. Customs were not allowed within 60 days of the request to inspect;

Three, by maintaining a list of suspected companies to make available to U.S. importers so they could avoid importing products from these companies; and

Fourth, requiring that bond be posted if a suspected company is used.

Additionally, Marck would suggest the following:

One, give domestic companies the ability to enforce the prohibition on importation of prison or forced labor goods into the United States;

Two, require that the name of the factory that produces the product be on Customs paperwork. Currently, a trading company can be listed as the exporter, and there is no way to know where the products were actually produced;

Third, if the importer of record's certification is challenged, a shift of burden to the importer to determine that the factory producing the product was not using forced labor in the production of the products and require it to assist in any inspection of the manufacturing facility by an independent monitoring agency.

Without swift and clear action by the United States Congress, American companies will continue to go out of business and American workers will lose their jobs.

Thank you again for this opportunity. I look forward to answering your questions.

[The statement follows:]

Prepared Statement of Mr. Gary G. Marck, President
G.G. Marck & Associates, Inc.
Toledo, Ohio

Members of the Commission and Staff, I would like to thank you for this opportunity to discuss the United States' Relationship with the Peoples Republic of China as it relates to the Importation of Forced Labor Products. My view reflects the experiences of an American Importer of Ceramic Products with first-hand, day-to-day knowledge of the ceramic industry in China and as a part owner in two ceramic factories in China. Additionally, I frequently travel to the manufacturing facilities in China to address issues related to the production and importation of ceramic products into the United States. Specific to this Hearing, I have knowledge relating to the importation of ceramic coffee mugs that were made in whole or part with prison labor.

G.G. Marck & Associates, Inc. ("Marck") was founded in 1986 to provide products to the drinkware decorating industry, mainly sold as promotional products. Marck has offices and warehouses in Toledo, Ohio and Mira Loma, California. Marck is a leading wholesaler of ceramic, glass, stainless steel and plastic products to the drinkware decorating industry in the USA, with over 2000 customers. Marck sources products domestically as well as imports from China, India, Thailand, Taiwan, Columbia, Turkey and France. In 2004, in an effort to avoid its loss of its source of ceramic products, Marck bought a minority interest in two Chinese ceramic factories.

During this hearing, I would like to highlight the difficulties faced by U.S. Companies that comply with the laws of the United States by importing products from factories that do not use forced or prison labor in the production of their products. Many foreign exporters and some U.S. importers ignore U.S. laws to gain a competitive advantage, albeit an unlawful one. The law abiding companies must choose to exit the business because the price in which the product is sold cannot be matched by lawful means or join in the unlawful importation of products from prison factories. Additionally the Chinese and American agencies responsible for enforcing the laws and regulations have not taken adequate measures to ensure that all competitors have met those laws and regulations. Ultimately, without the assistance and intervention of the responsible Chinese and U.S. governmental agencies, law abiding companies both in the U.S. and in China will continue to go out of business and cease to exist. The loss of these law abiding companies impacts the

Unites States through its loss of tax revenue and American workers because of the loss of jobs.

Marck has knowledge, from a variety of sources, including eyewitness evidence, that ceramic coffee mugs produced at the Luzhong Prison of Shandong Province ("Luzhong") are being exported to the U.S. Since it is against Chinese Laws for prison made goods to be exported, the goods made at Luzhong need to be exported by another company. The Shandong Zibo Maolong Ceramic Factory ("Maolong") is the "front" for Luzhong. Details of our investigations have been provided to the Commission.

There are two separate prison camps for Luzhong. One is for hard core, long term prisoners and the other is what is referred to as a Re-education thru Labor Facility (RTL). It may be semantics, but the Chinese do not call this a prison. It is a Re-Education through Labor Facility that houses political and other petty criminals that are rehabilitated through work. It is this RTL facility that makes the coffee mugs.

Maolong is a small facility just outside the main gate of Luzhong. It has limited capacity to manufacture mugs. I do not believe it has ever made mugs. It is the "front" company used by Luzhong to export its mugs to the U.S. In order to get those goods to the U.S. there has to be an importer. A number of U.S. importers are importing mugs made at Luzhong and exported by Maolong. Most of these importers are aware of the Luzhong-Maolong relationship but chose to ignore the fact that prison labor was used to make their mugs because of the price advantage they receive.

This relationship unlawfully benefits the three parties involved. Maolong makes profit from the exports of the Luzhong mugs. Shandong Province benefits as they make profits from the prison (RTL). Lastly the U.S. importers that purchase the mugs from Maolong benefit from the low cost prison made mugs.

The losers are the Chinese and U.S. companies that compete with these prison made goods, ultimately causing the loss of jobs. China also loses as the prisons do not pay taxes as do the voluntary labor ceramic factories, so once Maolong drives all the other ceramic factories in China out of business they will have no tax income. Each year the number of viable manufacturing facilities decline because they can't sell their product at the same price as the prison made product and still remain profitable. Finally, the United States loses tax revenue directly related to the closing of businesses that can't compete with prison made goods.

It is Marck's belief that by increasing agency and private parties remedies available, there will be a significant increase in the effective enforcement of existing laws and regulations prohibiting the entry of prison made goods into the U.S. market. Marck submitted suggestions and concerns to this Commission on March 18, 2008 in a written statement about "China's Expanding Global Influence: Foreign Policy Goals, Practices and Tools", a copy has been provided. Additionally Marck appeared before the International Trade Commission's Investigation; "China: Government Policies Affecting U.S. Trade in Selected Sectors" testifying to the effects of prison labor on its business and how importation of prison made goods amounts to an unlawful government subsidy.

Marck strongly favors the recommendations made by this Commission in its May 3, 2002 letter to the Senate Finance Committee, suggesting that enforcement would be significantly enhanced by:

> 1) Requiring the importer of record to certify that goods were not made by prison labor;
>
> 2) By blocking imports from facilities where inspections by U.S. Customs (CBP) were not allowed within 60 days of the request to inspect;
>
> 3) By maintaining a list of suspected companies to make available to U.S. importers so they could avoid importing products from those companies; and

4) Requiring that bond be posted if a suspected company is used.

Additionally Marck would suggest the following:

1) Give domestic companies the ability to enforce the prohibition on importation of prison or forced labor goods into the United States.

2) Require that the Name of the Factory that produced the product be on Customs Paperwork. Currently a Trading Company can be listed as the Exporter and there is no way to know where the products were actually produced.

3) If the importer of record's certification is challenged, shift the burden of proof to the importer to demonstrate that the factory producing the product was not using forced labor in the production of the product and require it to assist in any inspection of the manufacturing facility by an independent monitoring agency.

Without swift and clear action by the United States Congress, American companies will continue to go out of business and American workers will continue to loose their jobs.

Thank you again for this opportunity and I look forward to answering any of your questions.

COMMISSIONER VIDENIEKS: Thank you.

Mr. Ellis, please. I forgot to give you the guidelines. It's roughly seven minutes.

STATEMENT OF MR. DANIEL T. ELLIS, PARTNER
LYDY & MOAN, LTD., TOLEDO, OHIO

MR. ELLIS: That will just make me talk faster. Good morning. Members of the Commission and staff, I appreciate this opportunity to discuss the United States' relationship with the People's Republic of China as it relates to the importation of forced or prison-made goods into the United States and the difficulties faced by law-abiding companies that comply with the laws of the United States by refusing to import products made in whole or part by forced or prison labor.

My comments predominantly relate to Marck & Associates' attempt to investigate the unlawful importation of ceramic products made by forced labor into the United States and its efforts to stop the practice so that the competitive commercial marketplace is not lost.

My statements reflect the experience of Marck & Associates over the past three years in its attempt to shine light on the ceramic products imported from Maolong and Luzhong related prison facilities.

Mr. Marck explained that Shandong Zibo Maolong Ceramic Factory is the front for Luzhong Prison of Shandong Province. Luzhong is a state-owned prison facility that produces 70 million pieces of ceramic products per year. The importation of ceramic products manufactured at a prison labor facility such as Luzhong offers a price advantage that cannot be met by companies complying with the laws of the United States.

The inability of the United States and legitimate companies to stop the importation of prison-made goods undermines the long-term stability of companies and the competitive marketplace in America.

In 2005, after Marck confirmed that one of its competitors was engaging in unfair business practices including importing ceramic products produced by prison labor, they filed a lawsuit captioned G.G. Marck & Associates, Inc. v. James Peng, Photo U.S.A. Corporation, North American Investments Corporation, and Photo USA Electronic Graphics, Inc., in the United States District Court for the Northern District of Ohio in the Western Division.

One of the competitive advantages obtained by the defendants was they obtained the ceramic products from Maolong/Luzhong below the price in which Marck could obtain and import a similar product from a legitimate commercial factory.

Although the court awarded damages to Marck in excess of $1.5 million including sanctions for defendants' willful violation of a permanent injunction related to various unfair trade practices, it concluded Marck had not met its evidentiary burden of proof that ceramic products introduced into evidence came from the Luzhong Prison.

The causal connection that the mugs introduced into evidence from Maolong were manufactured at Luzhong was frustrated by Chinese classification of the information as a state secret. Any witness brought to establish the connection would have been subject to being accused of disclosing classified information and would have faced criminal prosecution.

On August 9, 2006, Marck also made a formal request to the U.S. Customs and Border Protection to conduct an investigation into what it believed was the illegal importation of ceramic products manufactured at the Maolong/Luzhong prison facility in the United States from China for commercial use and resale in violation of 19 U.S.C. Section 1307. That section actually precludes the importation of prison-made goods in whole or part.

Marck is aware that the U.S. Customs and Enforcement has requested information from the Ministry of Justice, the People's Republic of China, under the Memorandum of Understanding on their relationship between Maolong and Luzhong so that Customs can investigate and withhold the release of the prison-made goods if warranted.

As of the date of this hearing, it is Marck's understanding that the information has not been provided to ICE.

On April 5, 2007, Marck filed a third-party complaint with the Fair Labor Association, alleging a code of conduct violation at the Maolong ceramic factory. Marck also asked that the FLA initiate a certified independent factory audit to confirm the relationship between Maolong and Luzhong Prison.

Marck outlined the facts supporting its contention that Maolong is the front for the Luzhong Prison. The FLA declined to accept Marck's complaint for review for procedural reasons, unrelated to the merits of Marck's complaint, because according to its charter, a Category C licensee is required to own or operate the factory.

Despite the FLA's concluding that at least one Category C licensee was being supplied by Maolong and Luzhong, it determined the complaint did not meet the requirements for initiating a third-party complaint.

The FLA did inform the FLA's university liaison, Heeral Coleman, so she could be in contact with relevant Universities and Colleges.

If Congress or American companies are relying upon the FLA to monitor factories in China to comply with its code of conduct relating to prison labor, their trust is sadly misplaced.

Additionally, Marck requested the Workers Rights Consortium to conduct an independent audit of the Maolong/Luzhong Prison to evaluate whether they are related entities. The WRC has conducted an investigation but has not yet released its report.

It is our belief that the WRC will ultimately conclude that Maolong and Luzhong Prison are related entities.

As a direct consequence of Marck's efforts to show the relationship between Maolong and Luzhong Prisons, the markings on the cartons of imported ceramic products are being falsified to obscure the factory in which the product has been manufactured.

Marck has observed cartons that do not identify the factory which produced the ceramic products, cartons in which the Chinese Commodity Inspection Bureau number does not match the factory labeled on the carton, or the use of the CCIB numbers of factories no longer operating.

The CCIB number is a requirement of importation of ceramics under the Memorandum of Understanding between the Food and Drug Administration and the People's Republic of China's Administration pertaining to safety of ceramic tableware.

It also appears that trading companies located in China are intentionally mislabeling the products so Maolong is no longer identified as the manufacturer or the exporter.

Marck strongly favors increased enforcement efforts and makes the following recommendations in whole or part to strengthen the

United States' ability to prevent the importation of prison-made goods:

Prohibition of the importation of any good produced at a factory identified in the Laogai Handbook by the Laogai Research Foundation unless the importer of record comes forward with independent certification that it is not a factory utilizing prison labor;

Require the importer of record to certify that goods were not made with prison labor;

Prohibit the importation of any goods from a factory that U.S. Customs is not permitted to inspect within 60 days of a request or that the Ministry of Justice, People's Republic of China, has not certified is not a front for a prison or related to a forced labor facility within 60 days;

Grant to companies a private right of action to initiate and enforce custom regulations including the prohibition on the importation of goods produced with prison labor. Require the initiating party to notify the U.S. Customs and Enforcement Agency of the filing of the complaint and provide the agency with the right to take over the case within 60 days of filing;

Require the U.S. Customs and Immigration Enforcement Agency to provide a governmental witness to certify that a factory is or is not related to a prison factory in any civil law suit;

After a preliminary or prima facie showing that a factory utilizes prison labor, shift the presumption and burden of proof in any civil lawsuit to the importer to demonstrate that the factory is not related to a prison factory;

Require all manufacturing facilities to be identified on the carton and the import documentation provided to Customs so that it can be checked against the Laogai Handbook or any other applicable list of prison factories in China;

Define use of forced prison labor in whole or part as an unfair business practice as a matter of law under the Lanham Act.

Domestic and foreign companies importing products in the United States through lawful means need immediate assistance to preserve the competitive marketplace and stay in business.

American workers are competitive with foreign workers if the competitive market is not undermined by the importation of goods manufactured by prison labor facilities. Swift and decisive action is required to preserve American jobs and domestic companies by leveling the competitive marketplace.

Thank you for the opportunity to highlight some of the difficulties being faced by domestic companies in their effort to compete in the global marketplace.

[The statement follows:]²

PANEL I: Discussion, Questions and Answers

COMMISSIONER VIDENIEKS: Thank you very much.

I'd like to open up with some questions. Commissioner Wessel, you have a question?

COMMISSIONER WESSEL: Yes, I do. Thank you for being here, gentlemen. Harry, it's good to see you again.

Your case study provides some enormous information for us and it's appreciated. I'd like to understand. Your self-help approach is laudable but expensive. I assume you are not a Fortune 500 company. I don't know that, but thus the resources you have to expend to try and protect your company's interests are scarce and many others I'm sure are not willing to expend similar amounts.

Can you tell me what kind of cooperation you've gotten from your own government as you've done this? What priority do you think our own State Department places on enforcing the agreement that, in fact, it negotiated and, as Mr. Wu indicated, ten years later one of the investigations was done which was supposed to have been done within 60 days?

Give us some flavor of how you've had to go about this self-help measure, please.

MR. MARCK: As they say, you have to have principles and sometimes you get burned by them, but it has been frustrating for a number of years trying to comply with the laws of the United States and at the same time having your competition being able to hide behind this memorandum.

It's not enforceable and it's not--we had difficulty, as Mr. Ellis has said, proving in a court of law something that it's hearsay. You can't bring the parties. You can't go to the prison, et cetera.

We are looking at it from survival. We will eventually fail if we all we have--if our only competition is forced labor in China or any country. It doesn't matter what country it is. No voluntary labor can actually compete with prison labor.

COMMISSIONER WESSEL: But if you could, also, the question of what assistance your own government has given you? When you've come with this information, have you found any assistance from State Department or other entities?

MR. MARCK: No, no, very little. We have gone to U.S. Customs, and I've actually gone to Beijing and met with the ICE agent in charge. Okay. And they, I think they are frustrated too. They

---

² **Click here to read the prepared statement of Mr. Daniel T. Ellis**

don't have the ability to investigate these issues. So--

COMMISSIONER WESSEL: They've put it way down the priority list.

MR. MARCK: Yes, and I think terrorism and other issues are higher on the agenda, and I have no objection to that, but these are issues that need to be addressed, but U.S. Customs is now Customs and Border Protection and it's Immigration and Customs. It's all meshed together. Homeland Security and 9/11 issues and child pornography issues have a higher rating that ceramic coffee mugs being made with forced labor in China.

COMMISSIONER WESSEL: I understand. Mr. Ellis, as a legal matter--and it's been some time since I've looked back through the Tariff Act and all its, the antecedents--an importer is a broad term and not subject to a very discrete definition.

If an individual, a U.S. individual, goes over, for example, to the Olympics this summer and were to purchase an item on the street, one of these mugs, one of the mascots or anything else that might be the product of prison labor, my understanding reading through all of the materials that we've been provided in the basic statute is that individual, in fact, could be in violation of the law for importing a product made from prison labor.

Would that be your reading as well?

MR. ELLIS: I think that you have to have a commercial purpose.

COMMISSIONER WESSEL: Okay.

MR. ELLIS: So if you just bought it and brought it back, I think you'd be okay. But you don't have to look that far. All you have to do is go down to the coffee shop down here and look at the mugs in there, and if you look at the bottom of the mug, it says "Decorated in the United States." It has no country of origin mark. It violates the United States law.

COMMISSIONER WESSEL: You're saying in our own shops here?

MR. ELLIS: Yes, if you just go right downstairs where I got coffee this morning.

COMMISSIONER WESSEL: So the U.S. Senate might be in violation at this point.

MR. ELLIS: They are. There's no country of origin marked that discloses to the ultimate purchaser of the mug, which is whoever bought that mug, where that mug came from.

The inference is, because it's decorated in the United States, it came from somewhere else, but where? Since it's a ceramic coffee mug, if the FDA had to go trace back the cadmium or lead content because it is in excess of the limits, how does it do that when it's not been identified on the mug?

COMMISSIONER WESSEL: Okay. Thank you.

COMMISSIONER VIDENIEKS: Mr. Slane.

COMMISSIONER SLANE: Mr. Ellis, first, I want to thank you for taking the time to come here.

The real problem here is the causal connection; is that a fair statement?

MR. ELLIS: Yes, it is.

COMMISSIONER SLANE: I'm struggling to try to figure out a simplistic solution here. Can we recommend to Congress that if there are mugs being sold at prices that are noncompetitive, that the burden shifts to the importer at that point?

MR. ELLIS: Yes. If you just took the position that after the United States government has asked the People's Republic of China under the Memorandum of Understanding to identify whether the facility is a prison, and they refuse to give the information--like Harry said it took ten years-- after 60 days there's a presumption that the facility is a prison factory until you come forward and establish it is not.

In a court of law, if that's what you're asking, that is the most difficult thing for us to prove because there's indirect shipment. There is no direct shipment from Luzhong to the United States. I mean the Chinese government bans that. The United States government bans that.

So what you have is trading companies coming into existence. Maolong and others who buy directly from the factory, import it into the United States, remark it, relabel it sometimes, mislabel it sometimes in order to hide the connection to the Luzhong Prison. And so if, and that's why I suggested in my closing statement that if you, as an evidentiary issue, require the U.S. Customs to come forward and say I requested and they didn't provide the information, so there's a burden shift and a presumption that it is forced labor.

The importer is in the best position working with the factory to get it certified as not a forced labor facility. That's why we asked the FLA to do an independent audit because if you go in and you look at Maolong, they don't have the mills to process the clay. They don't have the facilities. They don't even have any purchase orders for clay. It all comes through the prison.

They don't have storage facilities for their mugs. You can see they're stored inside the prison, so it's difficult to get the information. I can show that and say that, but the problem I encountered in my litigation was the defendants took the position, well, Maolong says they produce mugs too, and all mine came from Maolong, not the prison.

COMMISSIONER SLANE: The problem here is the only way

that this is going to be enforced is by private industry, people like Mr. Marck who will go after companies that obviously are violating the law here. It's amazing to me that you won the case in federal court with the causal connection issue, but shifting that burden would be an enormous help.

MR. ELLIS: It would, because the person that has the ultimate ability to confirm the causal connection is the importer because they're aligned in interest. The factory wants to import, the importer wants to import, and so if they independently go to a facility and, you know, like the Bureau Veritas has certified audits they can do establishing it is not using forced labor in any of its production or materials. In our case, they tried to get the Bureau Veritas to do a noncompliance audit.

And then they used that as, well, see, it doesn't use prison facilities, but the Bureau never looked at the prison issue. If you looked at even what the report said, they didn't look to see whether or not the raw materials came from another prison or any part of the product came from the prison facility, which as far as I can tell, given the investigation we had, it all comes through Luzhong, and I'm not sure Gary's right, whether they make mugs or they don't make mugs. They appear to be more of a decorating facility.

But they go under the cover of, well, jeez, we say we produce 70 million. If you look at their advertising materials, they will tell you they produce 70 million pieces. The prison also says they produce 70 million pieces.

The problem that Maolong has is that it only has one kiln and it can only produce ten million, and in a court of law what I asked the parties, well, where did the other 60 million come from, I have no idea, and so I don't have any idea either except that they're right across the street from a prison that has six kilns and can produce 60 million.

Now that isn't sufficient in a court of law because it's all hearsay and a lot of it was precluded from being introduced.

COMMISSIONER SLANE: Thank you.

COMMISSIONER VIDENIEKS: Commissioner Mulloy.

COMMISSIONER MULLOY: Thank you, Mr. Chairman. I want to thank all three of you for being here and giving us this very helpful testimony.

Let me just lay out what I understand and then you help me. We have a law on the books of our own country I think passed over 80 years ago that permits us to ban goods made by prison labor.

MR. ELLIS: They are banned. They can refuse the importation of them. They can stop it at the border.

COMMISSIONER MULLOY: Yes, we can keep them out of our country.

MR. ELLIS: Right.

COMMISSIONER MULLOY: Under that law. And when we entered the GATT and the WTO, we preserved the right to be able to use that law so it's permissible for us to ban those goods under the WTO.

MR. ELLIS: Right.

COMMISSIONER MULLOY: Now then the next question is why isn't the law being enforced? You guys say that there are goods coming in. Mr. Wu has documented this stuff in the past.

It appears that part of the problem is that the people who enforce these laws may have some other priorities from what you said, Mr. Marck. So what you recommend then is a private cause of action that the people who are injured competing with these be able to bring.

Now, my understanding is under our antitrust laws, we do permit private causes of action by people who are injured by antitrust violations. The government is not the sole enforcer. Is that your understanding, Mr. Ellis?

MR. ELLIS: Yes, and it's true under the Lanham Act too, like part of the reason we prevailed in the underlying action is under the Lanham Act if you don't put the country of origin on the product, there's a private right of action by individuals to enforce that.

One of the other competitive ways that they were getting an advantage over us was they wouldn't have a country of origin, and they could sell to any industries like we couldn't, like the United States Congress. When we try to sell to the Congress, they don't want "Made in China" on the bottom of the mug.

We can't do anything about that because it's required to be put on it so that if you just took the Lanham Act and added to that provision a private right of action saying that if you establish that prison labor is used in whole or part, just like under 1307, then that's an unfair business practice too, and an individual who is being harmed from that can recover damages.

I would suggest that, in revising the Lanham Act, you make the damages all of the imports because they're contraband.

COMMISSIONER MULLOY: I think you're going beyond my capacity right now.

MR. ELLIS: Okay.

COMMISSIONER MULLOY: We have a law that permits us to stop the stuff coming in.

MR. ELLIS: Correct.

COMMISSIONER MULLOY: You're recommending that we provide a private right of action for the enforcement of that law?

MR. ELLIS: That's right.

COMMISSIONER MULLOY: But yet you brought a case in the

District Court of Ohio and you won, at least part of it. That's what I don't understand. If you don't have a private right of action to enforce that law, on what basis did you bring that case in Ohio? Was it a different law?

MR. ELLIS: It has three aspects, well, there were four aspects in which we brought that case. We won three of them and lost the prison labor one.

COMMISSIONER MULLOY: You lost the case of the goods, that it was made by prison labor?

MR. ELLIS: Right.

COMMISSIONER MULLOY: You couldn't prove that.

MR. ELLIS: We couldn't establish the causal connection between the prison and the Maolong in the products that we had in the court.

COMMISSIONER MULLOY: Okay.

MR. ELLIS: It was clear--

COMMISSIONER MULLOY: Now that's not the Lanham Act.

MR. ELLIS: That's not the Lanham Act.

COMMISSIONER MULLOY: Okay. The Lanham Act is something else.

MR. ELLIS: But when you're engaged in--what we tried to do is, and it was a unique effort in which to try to enforce it because we faced the standing issue of you cannot enforce a private right of action to stop prison labor. That's a governmental function.

COMMISSIONER MULLOY: Right.

MR. ELLIS: You cannot stop lying to Customs on your transactional values because that's a governmental function. Those all have to be brought by the government in the Court of International Trade.

But the Lanham Act and some Ohio statutes provide for unfair competition, and what we argued was if you can utilize those acts to demonstrate the conspiracy to engage in an unlawful act to get a competitive advantage to the disadvantage of your competitors.

COMMISSIONER MULLOY: Okay.

MR. ELLIS: But, what ultimately happened was we have an injunction in place that precludes the importation of the stuff.

COMMISSIONER MULLOY: Let me just ask you one more thing because my time is coming to a close.

The simplified way to help you would be to provide a private right of action to ban the importation of the goods made by prison labor and then to fix the causal thing that Commissioner Slane was talking about.

MR. ELLIS: Exactly. If you say it's banned as an unfair business practice and shift the burden to the defendant to establish it's not, you fix the problem I had in court.

COMMISSIONER MULLOY: Okay. Thank you. We're going to have someone from the Customs Service come in here later and I wanted to get it clear what you wanted. Thank you.

COMMISSIONER VIDENIEKS: Commissioner Fiedler.

COMMISSIONER FIEDLER: Does anybody believe that the MOU is in any way effective? Mr. Wu?

MR. WU: If the American government really cared about the MOU, it would work. But since the MOU was signed, I have not seen any evidence of this. You see so many products made by prisoners. I cannot find any other country where the prisons make so many products. I found that Dun & Bradstreet lists every country including the United States, including India, including Japan. There aren't any prisons listed over there. But China has 314, and 396 are listed on the Dun & Bradstreet databases just as a prison name.

COMMISSIONER FIEDLER: 256.

MR. WU: Yes. This prison system provides big economic assistance. According to Chinese law, each prison system has two names. One is a prison name, indicating that it is a prison of the province, or of the city, and the other is the enterprise's name, such as a coal mine, or a manufacturer of whatever.

COMMISSIONER FIEDLER: I believe that Luzhong Prison was listed in your Dun & Bradstreet report, as well, I think.

Do you want to answer my question?

MR. MARCK: I would agree that the Memorandum of Understanding and the Statement of Cooperation because they're not enforced are useless and actually encourage people to take advantage of the situation, both exporters in China and importers in the United States, because there's no enforcement.

So if somebody was speeding down the road and there's nobody to give them a ticket, then nobody worries about the speed limit. So likewise, there's no enforcement.

COMMISSIONER FIEDLER: So, hence, you suggest private right of action. I understand that.

MR. MARCK: Yes.

COMMISSIONER FIEDLER: Now, let's talk about the 60-day requirement in the MOU and in the SOC, which apparently has not been lived up to even modestly, if I understand your testimony. There was in one case you cited, there was a ten year gap between the request for the visit, and in documents that I've been looking at, I don't think I see anything quicker than five years where the agreement says 60 days.

So the question then becomes on a political basis with the United States, it seems to me, how do you create an environment where you get compliance with the 60 day thing? For instance, perhaps by refusing entry to that product until a visit is allowed, which is, it seems to me, our power to do, legislative power certainly to do, to require.

I think it would require legislative power. We'll ask ICE that. It may not. It may be only administrative detention because they currently, by the way, it seems to me, you've gotten detention orders in the past that are not the same level of evidence that you were required to meet in court.

So we'll explore with ICE, I think, when they arrive, what the differences are in the evidentiary requirements because it seems to be you as a private individual or as a business have a higher level of evidence to meet than does the government when it denies entry to the product.

I see my time is running out.

MR. ELLIS: Can I just address that for a second?

COMMISSIONER FIEDLER: Yes, please.

MR. ELLIS: To deny entry is a lower burden, but once it's been denied, it's required to be appealed up to the Court of International Trade. And the Justice Department will face the same burdens I had.

There's a General Accounting paper that was published in 1995 regarding a memorandum of understanding that just suggests they're not sure they could meet that burden either. I mean they would have the same hard requirement I have to support what Customs has done without the cooperation of the Chinese government to identify the relationship.

COMMISSIONER FIEDLER: But there is a bit of a practical problem for the importer, is there not, that it would take him a little while to go through the International Trade Court procedure.

MR. ELLIS: Yes, that's why I suggest you--

COMMISSIONER FIEDLER: While his product is sitting on a dock somewhere.

MR. ELLIS: Right. It would, but, ultimately if you just make some very simple modifications. If you don't identify it in 60 days, then there's a presumption it is banned until you come forward and establish it is not produced using forced labor. That makes it simpler and they are in the position to get the information necessary to support that it's not or it is.

COMMISSIONER FIEDLER: Thank you. I'll come back.

COMMISSIONER VIDENIEKS: Commissioner Reinsch.

COMMISSIONER REINSCH: Thank you.

Commissioner Mulloy pursued the same line I was going to pursue to try to get a better understanding of the legal situation. I thought he got good clarification, so I'm going to confine myself just to a couple questions.

Mr. Wu, you've been involved in this as we all know for a very long time. How has the United States government's attitude or enforcement enthusiasm changed over time? Have you found some periods when the United States government took on this task more aggressively than it is now, or have you found it pretty much constantly in a state of disrepair?

And, in particular, have you noticed any difference from before and after the time that the Department of Homeland Security was created and the Customs Service was folded into ICE?

MR. WU: So far I know that, for example, a Chinese official from a Shenyang rubber boots manufacturer, he contacted me and he went to Vladivostok in Russia, and American officials, Customs officials from Beijing, went to Moscow to meet him, and get information, and give him the permit that would allow him to go to the United States to testify before the Congress.

But, unfortunately, later nothing happened. And the guy was rearrested by the Chinese and sent back to China, and we lost the connection. This is one case.

The other case was in 2000, the binding clips, because we had American enterprises here that violated the law, and the evidence was clear, and a witness also came to the United States. So that is the case.

Since then, I have not seen any activity related to the Customs Service in Beijing, what they did, particularly relating to the MOU. I have not seen any activities that followed the MOU regulations. So far they signed a paper; that's it. The SOC, they signed a paper; that's it. Only a paper.

COMMISSIONER REINSCH: Well, maybe Mr. Marck and Mr. Ellis, would want to comment, too.

My question is if there's a legal problem, and clearly we have a situation that's unacceptable from many different standpoints, it may be that the law is flawed and needs to be changed. But it may be that we just have a government that has a lack of enthusiasm for dealing with this problem. There are other ways to change that problem if you have people that are prepared to enforce it aggressively and use the tools that are available if those tools are adequate.

I'm trying to figure out if this is an enthusiasm problem or if you have inadequate tools on the face of it?

MR. ELLIS: When we submitted our request to Customs to investigate, they initiated an investigation. I would tell you that Customs is trying to do the investigation and are really hamstrung by the requirements on the Memorandum of Understanding to have the Chinese government or the prisons self-incriminate themselves. They can't get the information, and what they do is they delay giving the information or they don't give the information or they close the facility and then give the information ten years later when it's no longer operating.

So if you talk to the Customs investigators that are trying to do it, they're trying to do their job, but they can't get the information out of the Chinese system. The other factor that you need to understand is that sometimes I'm not even sure the Chinese government at the national level understands what's happening because Luzong is a state prison. It's happening in the province. They got enough other issues going on that sometimes that their focus isn't as clear.

COMMISSIONER REINSCH: That's a problem that we're familiar with. That suggests, though, that the terms of the MOU are inadequate.

MR. ELLIS: That's what I think. You could say as it's written and enforced, it isn't functional; it doesn't work. It's clear it doesn't work, and the question is, is there a way to fix it. I think there is, but it's giving the person like Mr. Marck the opportunity to stop it because he'll see it and do something about it, notify somebody, whereas the government may take forever. What you need to understand is a bunch of companies in America and in China have gone out of business in the three years we've tried to do this.

COMMISSIONER REINSCH: That's very helpful. Thank you. Mr. Marck, where do you make your products? Maybe I missed this in your statement.

MR. MARCK: In Shandong Province. I would buy products throughout China, but--

COMMISSIONER REINSCH: So what do you do in Ohio?

MR. MARCK: We're an importer and distributor. We distribute the products that we buy both domestically from Anchor Hocking, et cetera, glassware. We buy glassware, ceramics, stainless steel, plastic, that there's no decorations on them. They're blank, and we sell. We have at least 2,000 customers. The top 50 have at least a hundred employees that put the decoration on.

So if you wanted a United States symbol put on a mug, a ceramic mug, they would buy the blanks from me and then they would screen on the decoration and sell it. It usually goes to what we call promotional products, companies, businesses that want to advertise, a bank. We sell to secondary manufacturers. So we're an importer and distributor of drinkware products.

COMMISSIONER REINSCH: So if you shut down your operation tomorrow for the reasons you've been discussing, how many jobs in Ohio would be affected by that?

MR. MARCK: In Ohio, hundreds in Ohio and throughout the

country thousands because we sell throughout the United States and Mexico, Canada. We sell our products.

COMMISSIONER REINSCH: Yes, but wouldn't your customers just get them from a different source in that case?

MR. MARCK: Well, the only, oh, boy, our largest competitor is the prison factory. So they could get it from there as long as they're still producing. So I do have some customers that refuse to buy from them, but sometimes it's price.

We bring in product from Thailand, ceramic mugs from Thailand. We used to buy a lot from Japan. We used to even buy ceramic mugs made in the United States, but over time, the last few years, the price difference is such that they decided to exit the market.

COMMISSIONER REINSCH: Thank you. My time is more than up. Thank you.

CHAIRMAN WORTZEL: Commissioner Shea.

COMMISSIONER SHEA: Good morning. Thank you for your testimony.

Mr. Marck, I assume you're in partnership with a Chinese manufacturer; right?

MR. MARCK: In 2004, partially because of the WTO, a number of the ceramic factories in China, the government divested their interest in it, however you want to say it. Usually it was involvement from banks, and our largest supplier, our largest supplier of ceramic coffee mugs in Shandong Province was going to close.

The person I used to import my product in ceramic ware in China approached me and said they wanted to know if we want to help save this company, and we invested in that company to keep it going.

COMMISSIONER SHEA: But it's a majority owned Chinese company? The majority of shareholders are Chinese nationals?

MR. MARCK: Oh, sure, sure. Yes, yes.

COMMISSIONER SHEA: I'm just trying to get a sense of the extent of prison labor in China. Are there industries that are being ceded to prison labor, manufacturers, manufacturers who employ prison labor? I mean I assume it's not just an American ox that may be being gored, there's a private Chinese ox that's--

MR. MARCK: Sure.

COMMISSIONER SHEA: --getting gored here.

MR. MARCK: I know that in the last few years, there's been a number of ceramic factories that made coffee cups, dinnerware, et cetera, that have closed because they couldn't be competitive in China. There's less and less all the time and partially because of their competition. I don't care where you are, voluntary labor can never compete with forced labor on the same product, especially the more labor intensive.

In the ceramic industry, it's my understanding from the people I deal with that in the finished product, labor is 30 percent of a coffee cup. The labor factor. Again, as I say, the prison has to put something on that for that, but they don't have to put as much on as the voluntary labor. The guards still have to be paid and they get some income from the manufacture of mugs.

COMMISSIONER SHEA: So the Chinese manufacturers and suppliers who are producing the mugs or other items without the use of prison labor, are they just throwing up their hands and saying we give up? Are they pushing back? Are they doing anything to stop being undercut?

MR. MARCK: They're just closing. I don't know internally if they have an ability to complain.

COMMISSIONER SHEA: Okay. Thank you.

COMMISSIONER VIDENIEKS: Commissioner Fiedler.

COMMISSIONER FIEDLER: He was first, I think.

COMMISSIONER WESSEL: Thank you. I'd like to get some more clarification. Also, while we appreciate, Mr. Marck, your discussion of what you've done, there are, I'm sure, many companies here in America who are directly competing with products that are coming in, not just simply an importer of ceramic cups that are being etched or whatever else here, that there are basic products that are competing against basic manufacturers here. So this is a very broad problem.

I'd like to understand and appreciate very much the work that, Mr. Wu, you have done in matching this up with Dun & Bradstreet. I find it startling that we have well over 300 companies, prison labor facilities, that are on Dun & Bradstreet's list. That would appear to me to be an investigatory road map for our government to be able to start connecting the dots as to the competitive threat we're facing.

Have you met with our government about this? Are they aware of your work? What are they doing? And Mr. Marck and Mr. Ellis, what would you do? You've seen this work and you've referred to it as well. What can we do to utilize this work and start being more aggressive in fighting for American interests?

MR. WU: I never met any government officials. We just released this research today.

COMMISSIONER WESSEL: Okay. What would you do, Mr. Marck and Mr. Ellis, with this work? But, Mr. Wu, there have been numbers in the past regarding the Dun & Bradstreet numbers. It was a smaller number, as I remember, in the past, but this is a whole, a monumental increase in terms of the identification of these facilities, as I recall?

MR. WU: Since 1991, from my view, the Customs Service was

quite active. They issued a lot of detentions, product detentions by Customs, and took American enterprises that violated the law to court. But after a couple of years, I haven't seen any actions from the Customs Service working on it, particularly with regard to the MOU. They just signed it. You see that the prison visit took ten years. This is kind of ridiculous.

I feel that they don't really want to work on it because, according to our Foundation, so many products including garments, including mining products, including agricultural products, today they are indirectly exported to the United States--indirectly. But they did export them.

This is a facility that's in every Chinese prison system, yet, I did not find it in any other country listed.

COMMISSIONER WESSEL: Mr. Ellis, just with your legal knowledge, what would you do now that you have this information if you were a government official?

MR. ELLIS: Even with the Dun & Bradstreet information, they name the prisons, I mean that's the same as similar information that's in the Laogai Handbook. Those aren't the importers. Those aren't the front companies. Those are the prisons. And even if you have that information and even if the government has the information, you have to connect how are they getting it to the United States.

It's clear that they're getting it to the United States. The question is, and it's the problem that I had, it's all indirect. The Chinese government precludes the exportation of prison labor. The United States precludes the importation of it. Yet it comes here.

It's part of the expansion of China where you have entrepreneurial Chinese attempting to make a buck, and they'll push the limits on how they get that buck, and they'll say, well, it doesn't matter, nobody cares. Well, you do care, but we've been approached by trade companies, and I think I've submitted that information to you, that actually asked us to buy cups from them, and we asked them where they get them, they said Maolong, and we say, well, that's a prison facility, and they said, yes, but the price is cheaper so you ought to want it.

It's difficult. The legal system can't address the issue if you don't shift the burden or give us a private action. The government has the same problem as we do in the sense that the Chinese won't give them the information or the connection, and I don't know how Dun & Bradstreet is going to get the connection.

We're able to get it because Maolong is sitting on the front porch of the Luzhong Prison, and so you'd have to take those 350 companies named there and then try to find the front company because they all have fronts. I think Mr. Wu could give you more information on how the structure is set up in China because they all have front companies.

So that there is a system set up in which to export them, but it's never the facility named in Dun & Bradstreet.

COMMISSIONER VIDENIEKS: Commissioner Mulloy.

COMMISSIONER MULLOY: Thank you, Mr. Chairman. Mr. Chairman, I want to thank you and the staff who found this very capable group of witnesses to come in here and help lay out this issue. This is the best understanding I've had of this issue ever, and you three panelists have really helped.

Mr. Marck, you make the point that if the law isn't enforced, then the law-abiding companies either have to get out of the business or be tempted to also violate the law. That is correct.

It's because the law is not enforced, it allows businessmen that are willing to skirt the law to do it without a repercussion.

COMMISSIONER MULLOY: Yes. So that's driving down standards rather than--

MR. MARCK: That's right. That's right.

COMMISSIONER MULLOY: And sometime ago, our country put a law into place because we didn't want lower standards. We wanted to prohibit this practice of importing prison goods.

MR. MARCK: Yes.

COMMISSIONER MULLOY: I think, Mr. Ellis, you could help us with this. I worked up here a long time so I have some idea of the legislative practice. We need a narrow fix on the Law that prohibits prison labor. It should establish a private right of action. How would you do that? Also explain why it's needed

If you see a broader fix, I think you ought to give us that separately. In other words, you were talking about these unfair business practices. Do that separately with an explanation of why that should be supplemented. Sometimes you have an opportunity to get a narrow fix that you can't get with a broader fix.

MR. ELLIS: I think the simplest way is to--

COMMISSIONER MULLOY: If you could give us that in writing.

MR. ELLIS: Oh, I can do that in writing.

COMMISSIONER MULLOY: Yes, that would be better.

MR. ELLIS: It would be better in writing. Yes, I'd be happy to do that.

COMMISSIONER MULLOY: Yes, that would be very helpful. Thank you again for your very helpful testimony.

One last thing. I don't think we should be dependent upon the Chinese government to help us enforce our own laws, if they would, and we've tried the Memorandum of Understanding. It doesn't work so let's take control of our own destiny, pass our laws and enforce them.

That's my view.

MR. ELLIS: What our experience has shown is that American companies can compete in the global marketplace even against China where everybody thinks that Chinese labor is so cheap. I can give you a situation where Gary Marck three or four years ago was trying to figure out what was going on because his competitors were being in the marketplace, and we have one small sector where there's a coating placed on the mugs that we coated in America.

We sold the mug to a company in Colorado that had 50 employees that coated the mug and then sold it in the United States. What we found was in discussions with them was that something was going on, so we moved the coating operation to China, assuming, like most Americans would, the labor is cheaper.

When the Chinese coating factory fully operational, our competitors were still beating us in the marketplace, and that's what drew our attention to what's really going on, and what's really going on is through unlawful activities, Chinese companies are taking advantage of our inability or maybe will to enforce our laws and are getting a competitive advantage in putting American workers out of jobs and putting American companies out of business that could compete in the global marketplace if the level playing field was enforced.

COMMISSIONER MULLOY: Thank you.

COMMISSIONER VIDENIEKS: Commissioner Slane.

COMMISSIONER SLANE: To follow up with Commissioner Mulloy's suggestion, I think to get something done here, we need a very narrow definition. It seems to me, and help me here, that what triggers this shift of a burden is really the price.

If it's coming in here way below what it costs the manufacturer in China to make, then there's something obviously wrong. Is that a fair statement?

MR. ELLIS: If you take what I just said, is that we knew there was a price difference that we couldn't meet, and so we did everything a commercial manufacturer would respond to be competitive. We moved the facility. We tried to engage in all legally accepted conduct, and the answer is yes. But sometimes there can be advantages in the marketplace that we haven't adopted yet, and we will adjust.

But, the narrowest way that I can think of, just sitting here, is that once Customs asks for clarification of whether a facility is using forced labor, if they don't give an answer to them, it's marked as prohibited from being imported. I mean it's simple. It's already within the Memorandum of Understanding to ask.

COMMISSIONER SLANE: Okay. My other question is have you collaborated with your counterparts in other industries in the United

State that are affected by this prison labor, Christmas goods and clothing, et cetera?

MR. ELLIS: The only extent we've done that is really in the International Trade Commission where we're suggesting that the importation of prison-made goods is an unlawful government subsidy or support of industry, and in that particular hearing, there was multiple sectors of the Americans that were similarly testifying.

COMMISSIONER SLANE: So obviously the problem isn't confined to ceramics?

MR. ELLIS: It's not.

COMMISSIONER SLANE: Okay.

MR. ELLIS: By 300 companies that are importing products, you can see it's not.

COMMISSIONER SLANE: Right.

MR. ELLIS: We have a narrow experience that I can share with you.

COMMISSIONER VIDENIEKS: Commissioner Fiedler.

COMMISSIONER FIEDLER: I would just like to make a comment to Mr. Wessel's question that certainly that Dun & Bradstreet listing has a fundamental intelligence use for the Customs Service. We'll ask when they arrive this morning whether they have their own such list.

I don't believe there should be any expectation from anyone that the Chinese government is going to cooperate with us in providing incriminating information about its prison system's exports. Historically, it's trading companies, state-owned trading companies, that have been used to send the product into the United States. In your case, it's a private importer, but in a lot of cases, it has been a state-owned trading company.

Have any of those state-owned trading companies ever been sanctioned for being fronts for forced labor camps?

MR. ELLIS: No.

COMMISSIONER FIEDLER: Which when we have sanctioned Chinese companies for various things, much more serious, i.e., Iranian missile parts and stuff like that, but we seem to have the ability to determine what Chinese companies are doing when we want to, and we don't have that ability suddenly when we don't want to.

I don't have any other questions. I know that we're running out of time and our next panel is arriving.

COMMISSIONER VIDENIEKS: Thank you to the panelists for the very informative testimony. I second Commissioner Mulloy's comments and thank you very much again.

We'll take a brief recess before starting our next panel.

[Whereupon, a short recess was taken.]

OPENING STATEMENT OF CHAIRMAN LARRY M. WORTZEL
HEARING COCHAIR

CHAIRMAN WORTZEL: Good morning, ladies and gentlemen. Thank you, again, for being here at this hearing on prison labor and China's prison system.

As you know, the real focus that the Commission has on this is compliance with the agreements that the United States government has signed with the Chinese, and I know that your first panel talked about practices there. I was telling one of our staffers outside, my very first trip to China was 1979. It was a six-week trip. I was in the Army, but I got a little leeway to go with a graduate student group from the University of Hawaii and it was the geography department.

So we did six weeks, a week in each city that had a Chinese Academy of Sciences geography department. And, you get a little tour and we went to Zhejiang Province which is down along the coast inside from Shanghai. We went to the Longjing Tea Factory, huge expanse, and they showed us around, showed us how tea is grown, they showed us how the leaves are picked and roasted.

And it was nine graduate students. We looked around and we said how come everybody picking tea and roasting it is between about the ages of 12 and 16? And the answer was this is a labor farm; these are all juvenile delinquents who have been sentenced to reform through labor, and their job is to pick Longjing tea, which is dried and packaged for export.

So I don't know what the Longjing Tea Factory is doing today, but I can tell you that that was my very first experience with prison labor in China. It's a tough and difficult problem.

We're very pleased today to have Mr. James Ink from Immigration and Customs Enforcement to talk to us about the government's view on it, how the Chinese government is complying with our agreements, and the ability of the people that are in the embassy to actually go out and make sure that prison labor products are not being exported to the United States.

Mr. Ink went to Florida State University in Tallahassee, and he's got a degree in criminology, so he's been in law enforcement for a very long time, served with the Miami Shores Police Department, went to law school at the University of South Carolina, and was a Navy Judge Advocate General in Hawaii.

I don't know why he came to Washington from those two nice places, but he says he's going to Singapore, which I think he'll like.

He joined the Customs Service in 1993 in the Miami office, and now he does international work here. He's been the ICE Attaché out in

Frankfurt, Germany. So we have a very experienced law enforcement officer and an attorney and trial counsel, and we appreciate you very much taking the time to be here and the government and the department for sending you.

STATEMENT OF MR. JAMES INK
DEPUTY ASSISTANT DIRECTOR
INTERNATIONAL AFFAIRS, IMMIGRATION AND CUSTOMS
ENFORCEMENT, WASHINGTON, DC

MR. INK: Thank you, sir. Good morning, Chairman Wortzel and Commissioner Videnieks, distinguished members of the U.S.-China Economic and Security Review Commission.

It is my privilege to appear before you today to discuss Immigration and Customs Enforcement or ICE's role in the investigation of prison labor in China and the implementation of the Memorandum of Understanding between the United States and China regarding prison labor products.

I would like to thank the Commission for its continued commitment to combating prison labor in China. The importation of goods into the United States that are manufactured by prison labor is prohibited under the Tariff Act of 1930, or 19 U.S.C. Section 1307. Now, the Tariff Act is a Depression era legislation enacted during an era that focused on protecting U.S. agriculture and industrial interests.

Since then, the focus of prison labor investigations has evolved to become more concerned with the violation of human rights. Specifically, the law prohibits the importation of merchandise that is mined, produced or manufactured wholly or in part in a foreign country by convict, forced or indentured labor under penal sanctions.

Historically the United States Customs Service pursued allegations of importation of goods manufactured with forced, child or prison labor. However, in 2003, the Department of Homeland Security was created, and the United States Customs Services Office of Investigations merged with the Investigations Branch from the Immigration and Naturalization Service to form Immigration and Customs Enforcement, or ICE.

Since that time, ICE has assumed the legacy United States Customs Service's role of investigating allegations of forced, child and prison labor.

Investigating allegations of prison labor in foreign countries is the responsibility of ICE Attaché Offices abroad who operate out of the Office of International Affairs.

Currently, ICE has approximately 50 offices in 40 locations throughout the world. Attaché Offices are responsible for coordinating international investigations with foreign counterparts, providing support to our domestic offices, as well as other international ICE offices, and combating transnational crime, acquiring and developing intelligence related to cross-border criminal activity, and fostering lawful international trade and travel through liaison with host country governments, industries, and law enforcement.

In addition, the Attaché Offices are responsible for coordinating with foreign counterparts on sharing information under bilateral agreements such as Customs Mutual Assistance Agreements or what are referred to as CMAAs or Mutual Legal Assistance Agreements, such as MLATs. Actually they were often called Mutual Legal Assistance Treaties.

In 1992, the United States and China signed a Memorandum of Understanding prohibiting trade in labor products and allowing the ICE Attaché to inspect Chinese prison facilities to verify that Chinese prisoners were not making products that were being imported into the United States.

In 1994, a Statement of Cooperation was signed by the United States and China which clarified the procedures for investigations and prison facility visits.

According to these agreements, either party may request the other to promptly investigate companies, enterprises or units suspected of violating relevant regulations or laws based on specific information provided by the requesting party.

The agreement further stipulates that in order to resolve specific outstanding cases, each party will upon the request of the other party promptly arrange and facilitate visits by responsible officials of the other party's diplomatic mission to its respective companies, enterprises or units.

In 1994, after the signing of the Statement of Cooperation, ICE Attaché Beijing opened 12 prison labor cases based on allegations and information that we received. From 1996 to 2000, ICE conducted three prison visits and found no evidence to support allegations that goods manufactured by prison labor were being exported to the United States.

However, in February 2000, Allied International Manufacturing Company of Nanjing, China became the first company to be convicted in the United States for violating forced labor laws by transporting goods made by prison labor into the United States. That is the metal binder case if you're not already aware of it.

In June 2002, Treasury Assistant Secretary Kenneth Lawson met with the Ministry of Justice Director General in China, and following the meeting, relations between what I'll refer to as MOJ and ICE improved, and in September 2002, the ICE Attaché and other U.S. Embassy officials conducted the first prison visit since 2000.

From February to September 2003, MOJ and ICE Attaché Beijing held monthly meetings. There was a brief suspension of prison visits at that time due to a SARS, or Severe Acute Respiratory Syndrome, outbreak, but the monthly meetings resumed in 2004 and continued through June 2006.

During this time, ICE Attaché Beijing visited five facilities and, finding no evidence to substantiate allegations of prison labor, closed all five cases.

Today, ICE continues to work to pursue these cases. We believe it is only through a strong collaborative effort with full adherence to the terms agreed upon in the MOU that we can successfully investigate and stop importation of goods into the U.S. produced by Chinese prison labor.

I hope my remarks today have been helpful and informative, and I would like to take this opportunity to thank the Commission for its support of ICE and our law enforcement mission, and I'll be glad to answer any questions you may have at this time.

CHAIRMAN WORTZEL: Thank you very much.

Can you tell us how you're staffed out in Beijing or at the consulates to conduct these investigations or visits?

MR. INK: We have the ICE Attaché that is out there supported by other ICE representatives working with them, and we have Foreign Service nationals who work with us at the Embassy there in Beijing.

CHAIRMAN WORTZEL: Thank you very much.

PANEL II: Discussion, Questions and Answers

COMMISSIONER WESSEL: Thank you for being here, and I appreciate your testimony and your help.

A couple of questions, if I may. Where does this fit in the overall scope of relations and what is the assistance that the State Department gives you? You mentioned just a couple of moments ago, as I recall, that you were having monthly visits which stopped roughly two years ago; is that right?

MR. INK: In 2006, they stopped for a period of time due to the SARS outbreak.

COMMISSIONER WESSEL: Right.

MR. INK: Then they resumed.

COMMISSIONER WESSEL: And have stopped?

MR. INK: In 2006, they stopped. There was some confusion, I believe. What had happened is, and I think I talked to you at the previous time we met on this, there was a monthly Prison Labor Working Group meeting, and the Chinese officials stated that they were interested in conducting high level meetings with U.S. officials on administrations of prisons as per the Lawson agreement of 2002, to exchange methodologies, views concerning the administration of prisons.

At that point, the ICE Attaché Beijing responded that that was a different area. In other words, that fell under the Department of Justice and the Bureau of Prisons, and that these were two separate categories. However, at that point in time, the Ministry of Justice said that they were going to stop the visits until a visit took place.

My understanding is that a visit did take place to the United States, but not on the issue of prison labor.

COMMISSIONER WESSEL: So is there any current dialogue now with the Chinese government on the issue of prison labor imports into the United States?

MR. INK: Actually, in a very timely event, on Tuesday, the Attaché, this week, met with Ministry of Justice officials to discuss continuing operations looking into the old cases and current cases.

The meeting, there was nothing overtly outstanding that took place at the meeting. It moved slow there. However, they discussed some of the concerns. The Ministry of Justice, my understanding, indicated or one of the officials indicated, that there were, I believe, seven areas that they were responsible for, and that one of those areas was developing policy and rules for prisons within China. However, the actual administration of the prisons was handled at the provincial level.

COMMISSIONER WESSEL: So since 1992, if I remember, the MOU, they have now essentially asked for a redefinition of the process. Am I understanding you correctly that they're now saying that this has not worked correctly, and we want to do this a different way?

MR. INK: No, sir, I can't say that. I can say to you that they stopped it. There was some confusion, but I believe the Attaché Office put it back on course.

Now, I know there were several inquiries sent up. I believe we sent up an inquiry on a case on October 31, 2007. In December, we met with Embassy officials to discuss further action, and again in April of 2008, we reached out. We actually reached out to an additional or a new administration or new agency within China. I believe it's the Ministry of Health and Human Resources and Social Security.

It was created, I believe, in April of 2008 as part of a reorganization in China. It's a super agency, so to speak, and they deal with labor issues as a whole. So we reached out to them to discuss some broader issues.

However, they also advised us that they would rather wait until July of 2008 to further discuss it, but as to your question on whether or not that they have indicated that there is a restructuring, no, I don't believe that's the case, sir.

I believe simply that there was some confusion. I believe we have set it back on course. We had asked to meet again. We've had some inquiries, and they are just getting back into meeting now.

COMMISSIONER WESSEL: How many open cases are there from your point of view?

MR. INK: We have, I believe, 13 outstanding cases, one that is active. Now when I say 13 outstanding, they have gone to a certain point, and at that point, we are waiting for a response so they are put into a pending status.

COMMISSIONER WESSEL: What is the longest that you are waiting if you have 13?

MR. INK: From 1994. At the statement, after they were opened after the Statement of Cooperation was signed.

COMMISSIONER WESSEL: So the 60 days has been abrogated in all those cases?

MR. INK: The 60-day time limit doesn't seem to be a hard and fast rule, sir.

COMMISSIONER WESSEL: Okay. Hopefully, there will be another round. I'll yield to that point.

CHAIRMAN WORTZEL: With Commissioner Fiedler's permission, I want to follow up on one point that you raised, Mr. Ink. Do you know if you can tell us whether the Bureau of Prisons of the United States has actually followed up on that other request for discussions on prison management?

MR. INK: I cannot answer that with 100 percent accuracy, sir.

CHAIRMAN WORTZEL: But that could still be a blockage in your work?

MR. INK: I don't believe so. I believe the Department of Justice had followed up on that. I'm just not cognizant of everything that took place.

CHAIRMAN WORTZEL: Thank you.

MR. INK: Yes, sir.

COMMISSIONER FIEDLER: A couple of questions.

MR. INK: Yes, sir.

COMMISSIONER FIEDLER: Does ICE maintain a list of Chinese prisons?

MR. INK: I'm not 100 percent certain as to whether the Attaché Office does. I don't believe we do at headquarters, no, sir.

COMMISSIONER FIEDLER: Does anybody in the U.S. government maintain a list, to your knowledge, of Chinese prisons?

MR. INK: I am not aware if any of the other agencies such as Commerce or Labor do.

COMMISSIONER FIEDLER: Does anybody in the U.S. government maintain a list of suspect products that might be coming in from--

MR. INK: No, sir. I think we discussed this before. We are aware of certain products pursuant to the cases that we may open where those products are brought up as a topic of being produced, but I'm not aware of a master list.

I know that some of the different divisions are aware of certain things that they keep a close eye on because of patterns, but I can't swear to you that there is a main list of all these type of things.

COMMISSIONER FIEDLER: Are you aware that this morning Mr. Wu came and gave us a report that he produced that lists 314 Chinese prisons he alleges in Dun & Bradstreet's international databases, its commercial databases?

MR. INK: I was aware he spoke this morning, sir, but I was not present, no.

COMMISSIONER FIEDLER: Have you ever used Dun & Bradstreet as a source of information for Chinese prisons?

MR. INK: When I was a field agent, I used Dun & Bradstreet, but I haven't used it in a long time, sir, to be honest with you.

COMMISSIONER FIEDLER: We were reported on this morning that 65 of the prisons that he found in Dun & Bradstreet's listings in China actually had the term "prison" in them.

MR. INK: I believe that's wholly possible, sir. That would be another source of information that any of our field investigators would use to collect information, and like Dun & Bradstreet, there are dozens and dozens of various systems that we can use to pull up information in all different formats with all different names that may give us something, but not necessarily give us a solid lead.

COMMISSIONER FIEDLER: Are you aware of whether or not the United States government including ICE or any other government agency expends any intelligence resources on the question of whether or not a facility is a prison producing products for export?

MR. INK: Intelligence resources?

COMMISSIONER FIEDLER: Other than public open source information?

MR. INK: I'm not sure I follow exactly what you're asking, sir.

COMMISSIONER FIEDLER: Okay. Do we listen?

MR. INK: I would not know that, sir.

COMMISSIONER FIEDLER: Okay, let's take open source information. ICE is not allowed to wander around China on its own; is it?

MR. INK: No, sir; that is correct.

COMMISSIONER FIEDLER: So does it look at Chinese publications to see if they're publishing any information on Chinese prisons and/or Chinese prison products?

MR. INK: Do ICE agents?

COMMISSIONER FIEDLER: Anybody in ICE or to your knowledge anybody in the U.S. government who provides that information to ICE?

MR. INK: I can't speak of any agencies within the U.S. government. I don't have that first-hand knowledge, but I would imagine that any ICE agent who's conducting an investigation which delves into the area of prison labor would probably avail themselves of those resources if they existed.

COMMISSIONER FIEDLER: If they existed. But you don't have any knowledge whether they exist?

MR. INK: No, sir, I don't have that first-hand knowledge.

COMMISSIONER FIEDLER: Do you think the MOU is effective as an enforcement tool of U.S. law?

MR. INK: The Memorandum of Understanding and the Statement of Cooperation both could be effective if followed, let's say, to the 60-day limits.

COMMISSIONER FIEDLER: So how would you suggest that persuasive ability be exercised in order to get visits to prisons within 60 days?

MR. INK: I believe that continued dialogue at both our level as the Attaché in China as well as at senior levels through State Department and otherwise, heads of departments, such as--or senior officials such as when Assistant Secretary Lawson went over there, that we continue dialogue at those levels so that they understand and continue to understand the magnitude that we view this problem with.

And I think that we continue through that level to approach the MOU and just how important it is to us.

COMMISSIONER FIEDLER: So you don't think that either in the last 15 years, you have not engaged in that dialogue to encourage them to do the 60 days, or maybe it needs 20?

MR. INK: At the ICE level, at the Attaché level, sir, we are involved with discussions concerning the cases that we're investigating and other topics around that. Whether or not other than at the senior levels--and I believe the last time they actually took place at that level was 2002--now, I know in 2006, the Chinese did want to meet, but that was, as I explained to you, there was some confusion on exactly what they wished to discuss.

Do I think it's time for another senior official to be engaged in that level? I would think so, sir.

COMMISSIONER FIEDLER: So you believe talk, not leverage from the United States, is necessary in order to enforce the 60-day time limit?

MR. INK: I wouldn't rule out leverage, sir. I just don't know that I have the answers as to what specifically leverage would get the Chinese government to do something different.

COMMISSIONER FIEDLER: Okay. I see my time is up, and I'll take a second round. Thank you.

MR. INK: Yes, sir.

CHAIRMAN WORTZEL: Commissioner Mulloy.

COMMISSIONER MULLOY: Thank you, Mr. Chairman.

Mr. Ink, thank you for your long service to the nation in many different capacities.

MR. INK: My pleasure, sir.

COMMISSIONER MULLOY: And your colleagues from the department that you brought with you.

MR. INK: Yes, sir.

COMMISSIONER MULLOY: I'm going to go through a few things, and since we're limited in time, if we could just get my question out and get the answer and we'll move right through a series.

MR. INK: Very well, sir.

COMMISSIONER MULLOY: Thank you.

As s you pointed out, we passed this law in 1930. That is the law.

MR. INK: The Tariff Act, yes, sir.

COMMISSIONER MULLOY: That permits us to prohibit the importation of prison, of goods made by prison labor.

MR. INK: Yes, sir.

COMMISSIONER MULLOY: Your group has a responsibility of helping to enforce that law; is that correct?

MR. INK: Yes, sir. As I explained earlier, from the days of the United States Customs Service, ICE assumed the responsibilities of investigating allegations of violations under the Tariff Act. Customs and Border Protection also works with us in the enforcement of it where goods are being brought into the United States.

COMMISSIONER MULLOY: I see where you were an Assistant U.S. Attorney for awhile.

MR. INK: I was a Special Assistant, sir.

COMMISSIONER MULLOY: You prepare the cases that then Justice would bring.

MR. INK: As a Special Assistant U.S. Attorney?

COMMISSIONER MULLOY: No, in your current capacity. Your agency would prepare the case and then Justice could bring the case to prohibit the importation of those goods?

MR. INK: Yes, sir. Our criminal investigators if they have sufficient evidence and put the case together and the U.S. Attorney's Office accepts the case, then we would move forward against the individual who was charged with the crime.

COMMISSIONER MULLOY: What other laws does your organization also have the responsibility of enforcing?

MR. INK: I can say that when we're the U.S. Customs Service, I had over 500 laws. Now, with ICE, we've merged both the former Customs and now the former Immigration into ICE. We have a myriad of crimes ranging from money laundering, child pornography, strategic weapons, dual use commodities, human smuggling, human trafficking, textiles, IPR violations, a myriad of different areas that we enforce, sir.

COMMISSIONER MULLOY: Where would this be in the priorities of ICE? You've got so many important duties. Where would this fall in the rank?

MR. INK: In the hierarchy. Obviously, prison labor is part of the--we call the category Forced Child Labor, and I believe Forced Child Labor was put on it simply because of the catch of children.

But Forced Child Labor is a significant program within ICE. To show you just how significant it is, we've, since the transition, and we've started--let me step back a second--the international aspect of ICE was kind of the last portion in the transition once the agencies had merged to become ICE.

That being said, within the last few years, we put a very concerted effort to get the Forced Child Labor Program up to speed. We just conducted a very big conference in Singapore, and at the end of last year, we conducted a big one in Miami where we're getting our agents across the board, both Immigration and Customs that have merged into ICE, up to speed on issues of forced child labor.

We're also in the process of putting together material that we can release to our attaches as kind of force multiplier where they will be able to go to their foreign counterparts with materials that they will give them, kind of train them to then go out and conduct these investigations in their own countries.

COMMISSIONER MULLOY: Okay. Now, then the next step for me is to say you talked about a case, the binary metals case?

MR. INK: The binder--the clips.

COMMISSIONER MULLOY: Was that a prison labor case that you brought successfully against somebody?

MR. INK: It was a successful case. I don't have all the background on the case, but--

COMMISSIONER MULLOY: Did Justice bring litigation?

MR. INK: It would have been prosecuted by Justice, yes, sir.

COMMISSIONER MULLOY: Yes. And you guys prepared it?

MR. INK: I believe so, sir.

COMMISSIONER MULLOY: In which country? Was that China?

MR. INK: Yes, sir.

COMMISSIONER MULLOY: And it was a prison labor?

MR. INK: Yes, sir.

COMMISSIONER MULLOY: And you brought it. Okay. I used to be in the Justice Department in the Antitrust Division so I have some sense of this--that the private bar could also assist in enforcing the antitrust laws. There's been a recommendation here that the private sector also be entitled to enforce the law that prohibits the importation of prison-made goods. I don't know whether you're free to opine on that or not.

MR. INK: As to whether or not the foreign or the private industry, I would leave that up to the legislation to make that determination. However, I can say as to criminal sanctions or criminal violations, I would suggest that it was the U.S. government.

COMMISSIONER MULLOY: No, it wouldn't be criminal enforcement. It would be to just to help enforce the ban so if somebody is bringing it in, that they could bring an action in the private sector to help prevent that good from being imported.

MR. INK: We stand ready at any time to take information from the private sector that would assist us with our investigations, and whether or not a criminal prosecution results from it or an administrative seizure, we would gladly take legitimate information and explore it to see whether or not there is something there.

Whether or not the private sector is situated to fairly be involved in whether or not goods are brought into the United States, I can't say although one would think that there might be some conflict of interest at times from a private industry regulating private industry where competitors are involved.

COMMISSIONER MULLOY: Thank you, Mr. Chairman. I think I'll just have to come back. Thank you. Thank you, Mr. Chairman. Thank you, Mr. Ink.

MR. INK: Yes, sir.

CHAIRMAN WORTZEL: Commissioner Videnieks.

COMMISSIONER VIDENIEKS: Good morning, again. The question I have follows up on Commissioner Mulloy's question. Can you be more specific as to the priority of enforcing the law prohibiting all imports containing prison labor? I understand terrorism is big right now and other things. Where would enforcement of it in the scheme of things, especially when you only randomly inspect like two percent of all imports coming in at the border or at the point of destination?

Okay.

MR. INK: You'll forgive me if I can't give you the exact numerical list, where it would fall on the list, but I know it is one of the significant programs within ICE given the amount of resources.

Now, again, when you say prison labor, I include that under the Forced Child Labor Program.

COMMISSIONER VIDENIEKS: Do you distinguish between what we call prison labor? The MOA and the SOC specifically talk about prison labor. Forced labor, Commissioner Fiedler is much more familiar with the subject distinguishing the two terms.

MR. INK: The money that we receive from the government for Forced Child Labor covers all the forced labor areas. So there are different subcategories of forced labor, but it is all part of, again, what I refer to as the Forced Child Labor Program or Forced Labor.

We take it seriously. We have several offices that are funded by the money to look at these type of issues, whether it be prison labor or slave labor in the various countries. We take it very seriously. We have several investigative projects that we work on and educating both our attaches and the foreign governments that we work with.

COMMISSIONER VIDENIEKS: We're not being country specific here, but the Commission's mandate is country specific.

MR. INK: Understood, sir.

COMMISSIONER VIDENIEKS: The question was asked earlier about staffing in Beijing. How many people does ICE have currently--

MR. INK: In the Beijing Office?

COMMISSIONER VIDENIEKS: --in the Beijing Office and who are, I guess--

MR. INK: Criminal investigators?

COMMISSIONER VIDENIEKS: Well, no. People dedicated to the narrow issue we're talking about here.

MR. INK: If I might?

COMMISSIONER VIDENIEKS: Yes.

MR. INK: Okay. We have two Foreign Service nationals, three ICE reps, and one assistant attaché and then the attaché.

COMMISSIONER VIDENIEKS: Thank you very much. The other question I have is about determination. You used to have a determination that had to be made at the commissioner level or even higher.

MR. INK: In the Customs Service.

COMMISSIONER VIDENIEKS: At old Customs prior to issuance of these detention orders. Is the level, the requirement for a determination at fairly high levels still in effect, and does it slow things down?

MR. INK: For the detention orders?

COMMISSIONER VIDENIEKS: Yes.

MR. INK: That would be handled by Customs and Border Protection, sir.

COMMISSIONER VIDENIEKS: Okay. Sorry.

MR. INK: No, that's okay. Believe me, since the split, it's--

COMMISSIONER VIDENIEKS: Things have changed.

MR. INK: Yes, sir.

COMMISSIONER VIDENIEKS: Thank you very much.

MR. INK: Yes, sir.

CHAIRMAN WORTZEL: Commissioner Slane.

COMMISSIONER SLANE: Thanks for taking the time to come here, Mr. Ink.

My question is when you are interacting with the Ministry of Justice, is it fair to say that they're really stonewalling ICE?

MR. INK: Having not taken place or having not been present during any of the negotiations and just dealing with the literature and material and reports and people I talk to on it, I would say that some of it is the way of doing business in that part of the world, and negotiations at any time between different countries can be slow and methodical.

When I was in Europe, I found the same thing. Whether it's any greater there than anywhere else, perhaps. Are they stonewalling? I can't give you any certainty on that, sir. I don't think I have enough empirical data. I mean I can tell you that things are not moving as fast as we would like.

COMMISSIONER SLANE: Let me ask another question. Do you see a disconnect between the Ministry of Justice and the provincial leaders where these prisons are located?

MR. INK: That would have been my next thought to your first question, that when they met on Tuesday, and the representative from the Ministry of Justice indicated that we are responsible for policy and regulations. But it is the provincial governments that actually handle the prisons and the investigations, our representative or our attaché requested information on a specific case that they brought up, which they said was unsubstantiated.

When we asked for the paperwork on it, his comment was that he did not have that from the provincial authorities and was not ready to discuss it any further. Could that be a stumbling block? I would say absolutely. As in any bureaucracy, and we've seen it in our own, at times information going from one agency or one level of government to the next obviously slows it down.

Given the size of the nation that we're talking about, I would say that that probably does have significant bearing on the speed with which this whole process was taking effect.

COMMISSIONER SLANE: Thank you.

CHAIRMAN WORTZEL: Mr. Ink, I'm not going to subject you to more than two rounds, but I think we do have time since you're the only witness and I know commissioners have questions. So if you'll bear with us.

MR. INK: Not a problem.

CHAIRMAN WORTZEL: We'll run through another round.

MR. INK: That's okay, sir. That's why I'm here.

CHAIRMAN WORTZEL: I'm going to start. I'm looking at the, I don't know if you've seen it, but the May 20, 2008 report by the United States Embassy on Forced and Child Labor that they did in response to a request from the Department of Labor.

MR. INK: I would have to say that I have not seen that, sir.

CHAIRMAN WORTZEL: You have not. Okay. Bruce Levine is the Labor Officer; he's an Econ Officer at the Embassy. I've served with him there twice. He's a great officer. I know him. He did a very comprehensive report.

It has a number of places in it where the drafters from the Embassy cite reports by former prison inmates of prisons attached to industries in China where goods were manufactured.

MR. INK: Yes, sir.

CHAIRMAN WORTZEL: Now, it's not your issue, but it's a little deficient in actually naming the prisons or the industries, which would be nice to have. And the cable is also a little deficient, I would say, in telling us where the goods go when they're produced because if they're not coming to the United States, not much of a problem for us.

MR. INK: I can't speak to the completeness of a State Department document. I would suggest to you, though, that if they left out names of prisons, allegations without more substance could subject the U.S. government to possible litigation should we erroneously state the allegation and it be proven false when that would come back on a company that was involved in goods or of some nature.

CHAIRMAN WORTZEL: I agree. I'm going to support something Commissioner Fiedler was approaching. I think we could probably debate how to prioritize prison labor versus moving nuclear materials to terrorists in terms of our national security priorities. Do you know if your Attaché or your people out there are involved in debriefing these prisoners or these former prisoners?

MR. INK: In China, it's a little difficult. We are not allowed to investigate in the traditional sense within China.

CHAIRMAN WORTZEL: But somebody at the Embassy is talking to a former prisoner.

MR. INK: I am not aware. I don't believe our people are. Whether or not someone else at post, I would find that would be a unique situation.

Now, if somebody was in the United States and they came forward with evidence to our offices that we could look into and investigate further, we would welcome them with open arms if they had information. But--

CHAIRMAN WORTZEL: We get out there once a year so we can actually pursue this out there.

COMMISSIONER FIEDLER: I know the answer to your question. CHAIRMAN WORTZEL: But I can tell you that as a Military Attaché at the Embassy, if the State Department officer drafted a report on arms sales, was in contact with some Chinese that was providing information, I'd probably be there.

MR. INK: Again, sir, within China, we are not conducting your traditional investigation. We certainly aren't doing it around town in China. Whether or not something goes on within the Embassy and somebody has spoken to us--

CHAIRMAN WORTZEL: Okay. Thank you.

MR. INK: Yes, sir.

CHAIRMAN WORTZEL: It's actually a pretty comprehensive report that they put in. Interestingly, the Chinese government, and they cite some efforts on the part of the Chinese government specifically to address child labor and that the Chinese government at least has told that with their own reorganization, that they intend to try and get better judicial review of forced re-education through labor. So decent report. I commend it to you.

MR. INK: Very well, sir.

CHAIRMAN WORTZEL: Thanks.

COMMISSIONER FIEDLER: After we met with ICE officials and your predecessor who was then I think an acting director.

MR. INK: He is the Deputy Director Michael Feinberg.

COMMISSIONER FIEDLER: Okay. You submitted some answers to our questions, and I'm wondering whether you have now changed positions from your testimony.

MR. INK: I believe the answers to those questions, we had suggested possible revisiting the MOU.

COMMISSIONER FIEDLER: Yes. You specifically say in response to questions about the 60-day issue, as a proposed amendment to the current MOU, ICE would recommend that if the MOJ, the Ministry of Justice, in China, does not respond within 60 days to a request, ICE would refer the case to CBP and recommend that CBP issues a detention order on all products entering the U.S. from that particular manufacturer.

That is a bit different and is a little in line with our previous witnesses' recommendations, which is if they don't let us in in 60 days, we don't let the product into the country.

MR. INK: I don't think it's necessarily different as much as additional. What was said there was in response to questions, specific questions, and it is a suggestion on revisiting the MOU and what might. To be honest, though, with you, sir, we cannot say for certain whether or not that is going to break the logjam, so to speak.

COMMISSIONER FIEDLER: No, the spirit in which it was asked, and I think given was that you folks are on the ground burdened with the responsibility of enforcing something that in our view or in my view certainly is an insufficient instrument and one in which you don't have the proper tools to do your job. And so we were not at all faulting ICE.

MR. INK: Understood, sir.

COMMISSIONER FIEDLER: We're faulting more the diplomats who foolishly, in my view, negotiated this agreement.

MR. INK: Far be it from me to stand in the way, sir.

COMMISSIONER FIEDLER: Now, the private right of action that was raised by Mr. Mulloy or earlier witnesses is clearly a civil action. All said and done, in the last 50 years or however long since Smoot-Hawley has been in, how many people have been put in jail under this as a criminal statute? Certainly not even six, I think, is a fair answer even though you probably don't know the exact answer; right?

MR. INK: All I could tell you is that I know in the binder case, the actual amount of punishment was relatively slight.

COMMISSIONER FIEDLER: I happen to have conversancy with the binder case because we in my other hat at the Laogai Research Foundation assisted the U.S. businessman in following the truck from its factory to the prison, back again, filmed it, went on television, blah-blah-blah, and you guys did a very good job because we got a witness out of the country into the United States at the risk of his life.

MR. INK: Yes, sir.

COMMISSIONER FIEDLER: Okay. And so it takes that level of evidence in order to put, rightfully so, someone in jail in the United States. We are quite different from China in that respect.

Therefore, it seems to me ineffective to have a criminal statute. The issue is not putting people in jail for violating our Smoot-Hawley law. The issues should be stopping the product from coming into the United States and stopping the practice on the other side of the ocean or disincentivizing another government to engage in this activity, not to put in jail greedy people only.

MR. INK: Yes, sir.

COMMISSIONER FIEDLER: And I think that's the basis for the private right of action that I heard, and the private right of action strikes me fixes the priority question, which is we have very important governmental priorities at the moment that pale the issue of prison labor, but individually, like our former witness here earlier this morning, is immediately damaged. He just doesn't get to the top of the priority list.

But he can take, if he is being put out of business by prison labor in China, he would have a private right of action if one existed in the law so that you wouldn't have to waste your time on prison labor issue.

MR. INK: Well, if I might. Again, we don't consider this a waste of time. This is what we do. We are criminal investigators and this is another one of the step--I understand where the private sector is coming from, but we take each of the laws that we enforce very seriously and do our best to cover as many of them as possible.

I understand that it may not be to the speed or liking of a lot of the private companies, but we do the best that we can. When the information is given to us by the private sector, we do our level best then to look and review every allegation, and if the evidence is there, we go forward on it.

COMMISSIONER FIEDLER: I don't think anybody here is faulting ICE for the doing of its job, but I would submit to you, and not in a glib fashion, and as an ending statement from me, that spending 15 years talking to these guys about getting things is characteristically a waste of time.

Thank you.

MR. INK: Sure.

CHAIRMAN WORTZEL: Commissioner Mulloy.

COMMISSIONER MULLOY: Thank you, Mr. Chairman. I want to follow up on what Commissioner Fiedler said. Here's the way I would understand. We have a law that says don't import this stuff. We fought then to make sure that that law was protected when we entered into the GATT and the WTO. In other words, we got specific articles in the GATT and the WTO that permit us to keep goods made by prison labor out of the country.

So our law is fully consistent with our international obligations. Then we had a problem in China, allegations, and I'm sure what happened here is the business community was concerned that if we're too rigorous in enforcing that law, maybe our exports to China could get hurt by them manufacturing cases. So everybody says okay, let's do an MOU, and the two governments will cooperate.

But the MOU doesn't work at least from what I can see. So then the question is businessmen in the United States who aren't bringing in the prison labor stuff suffer competitive disadvantage. Our own law is not enforced and it's a situation where the people say, well, if we're not enforcing the law, maybe we'll participate in the game.

The better way, it seems to me, is to bring the private cause of action on civil where then it's not a criminal matter; it's just businessmen helping to enforce the law. I know I asked you before and you were beginning to opine on that when we ran out of time. Please me through this based on your long experience what are the pros and cons, in your view, of amending the law to provide a private right of action?

MR. INK: I can't really speak to amending the law, and I would leave that to the legislature as well as my superiors. Again, going back to the private sector, I remember back when I was doing money laundering investigations within Miami, and often with what we call the "Black Market Peso Exchange, we had the business community come to us because legitimate businessmen were suffering where other businessmen were availing themselves of the Black Market Peso Exchange.

But they came to us in our law enforcement capacity to assist them, in other words, bringing us the evidence that these other businessmen were using unscrupulous tactics. They were breaking the law.

But I had not considered nor did they, I think, at that point in time giving them any kind of private right of action. Again, I can't speak for what the legislature should do. I won't presume to do that. There are conflicts, I believe, if private industry is a partner of ours and can help us in everything that we do, and in several areas private industry helps us with the seizures and the administrative sanctions.

But to whether or not they should have a right of action, again, one could see that a conflict of interest might arise within a community where one is tasked with some kind of right in enforcing or preventing violations.

COMMISSIONER MULLOY: Thank you. That's very helpful.

COMMISSIONER WESSEL: Let me pick up on just that matter for a moment and then go to one or two other questions because I think our trade laws are rife with private rights of action whether it's antidumping, whether it's countervailing duty, whether it's any of a number of other areas where the bar has the ability to petition bringing the case and have the halls of justice within our own government assist them in terms of pursuing American interests. So I think there are certain things that we may want to pursue in that area.

Let me understand a couple of things, and you said earlier that things are not moving as fast as we might like. That's probably the greatest understatement I've heard here.

Are the re-education through labor camps treated as prison labor by the U.S. government?

MR. INK: I can't speak to that--re-education camps. I would say we look at prison labor, prison facilities and prisons. So if something fell into what we considered a prison facility, and I assume that--

COMMISSIONER WESSEL: If they can't go home at night or they can't go home, we would consider it to be prison labor. So we're not willing to abide by the Chinese definition of what a prison is and is not; is that correct?

MR. INK: Pursuant to the terms of the MOU and what we're investigating, if we have reason to believe or an allegation that a certain facility that would rise to the level of a prison, in our eyes, I assume we would request the information pursuant to the MOU and the Statement of Cooperation as we would with a hard and fast prison.

COMMISSIONER WESSEL: Okay. Also, and correct me if I'm wrong, in my reading of the underlying statute, MOU, et cetera, as it's written now, if the Chinese do not respond within 60 days, we could detain the products at the border; is that correct?

MR. INK: I believe that is accurate.

COMMISSIONER WESSEL: And we simply choose not to at this point? In most cases.

MR. INK: There's a process that we have to go through where if we make the request, after a certain amount of time, they can file back with a request. Whether or not we choose to depends on the amount of evidence we have to substantiate an allegation or other factors that figure into it.

COMMISSIONER WESSEL: But you said there were 13 open cases, and I assume since we're continuing to pursue them, we continue to believe that there is some validity to those cases. As I read the underlying MOU and the SOC, as I recall, if one were to take this all the way out, that would probably be--what--120 days and maybe one other short period thereafter, certainly not 13 to 15 years?

MR. INK: What we are looking for would be compliance on the part of the Chinese with the MOU and the Statement of Cooperation in a response from them. This came up at the June 18 meeting where when the Attaché, during the conversation with the Chinese officials from the Ministry of Justice, the Attaché brought up or they had brought up, I think I told you, a case that they said the provincial government had looked at, and there was no substantial--it wasn't legitimate.

Our Attaché advised that we appreciated the information, but that we took these very seriously, and we needed a more formal response with information that we could work with, at which point we were told that they didn't have it. That was with the provincial and they weren't prepared to discuss it further.

So we indicated to them that we'd be filing a formal request in order to get that information. What we are looking for is them to come back and tell us no or yes. Now, shortly thereafter the Ministry of Justice official indicated that they knew that we had several cases that were old and open and that they believed that several of those cases involved companies where the production line had moved or the prison had shut down and that it was time to look beyond, maybe shut those cases down and move forward.

I believe our Attaché's response to that was that we could discuss closing some of these cases when we had received the requirements pursuant to the MOU. In other words, not a problem, we can move forward if you can provide us with the documentation saying one way or another as to these allegations.

COMMISSIONER WESSEL: Okay. But the earlier question I had asked is if under the MOU and the SEC, the time period lapses when we file a case, we would be within our rights to detain those products. We are being delayed by China's failure to respond in a timely manner. They are choosing at times to defer attention to provincial, local and other authorities. They don't seem to have the same problem with Internet freedom when they want to pursue something.

But this is at this point a question of bilateral unwillingness to pursue this, it sounds like to me as well.

MR. INK: I would have to look back, to be honest with you, with a certain scrutiny of the MOU and the Statement of Cooperation to ensure the exact requirements on that. Suffice it to say there is a 60-day requirement, but whether or not, I would have to look further as to what you're going into and alluding to, that we can go move to detain, because there's several other factors obviously that figure into whether or not we're going to, that Customs and Border Protection would detain goods, and again that is a different agency that makes the decision, whether or not to detain goods.

So, again, I would have to look further at it and I'd have to take other factors into consideration.

COMMISSIONER WESSEL: If you could look at that and get back to us, I'd appreciate it.

MR. INK: I will, sir.

CHAIRMAN WORTZEL: Sir, thank you very much for your forbearance, for sharing your time with us and your wisdom, and for your work for our country and your agency's work for our country.

MR. INK: Thank you very much for the time and, again, thanks for your commitment to this issue. I appreciate it.

[Whereupon, at 11:20 a.m., the hearing was adjourned.]